Table of Contents

Statement of Intent

I am not a trader and I am no investment expert, nor do I pretend to be. And I have no intention of selling this book as the ultimate financial solution that will make you millions in the blink of an eye, without lifting a finger. Why? Because, quite simply, such a thing DOES NOT EXIST.

THERE IS NO magic formula for making massive amounts of money in the stock market. THERE IS NO risk-free but hyper-profitable investment, and THERE IS NO fast track to becoming a millionaire without making any effort. There is no shortage of self-described "market experts" out there who will try to sell you infallible systems with ambitious names. Distrust them—they are only interested in clearing out your wallet.

However, some people make money every day in the stock market. Why? Because THERE ARE ways to intelligently pick the best investment solution that fits your personal situation. THERE ARE ways to keep risk under control. And THERE ARE statistically-winning strategies for long-term earnings.

In this book, I gather all I have learned over the years based on real experience in stock investment, and also on reading countless books, blogs, and articles on the subject. This book offers an overview of stock investment and in clear, accessible language will introduce you to how the Stock Exchange works. *Play Smart in the Stock Market – The 4 Keys to Success* will show you how to put your savings into production, how to wisely move your money to the best investment option each time, and how to make money work for you instead of you working for it.

Introduction

Based on foundational guidelines developed out of extended theory, logic, and practice, this book offers the reader a basic but discerning guide to making conscious, controlled, and intelligent investments in the Stock Exchange. These guidelines comprise four key pillars of successful investing:

1. Understanding the game
2. Defining your strategy
3. Picking winning horses
4. Managing risks

If you can build these four pillars into your investment practice, you can begin investing with confidence of success. The rest is just practice and experience!

"Understanding the game" means grasping the operation and functioning of the Stock Exchange and its secrets. This means knowing in depth which products are sold and bought and when, how and why their prices change, and how to access these products and the expenses involved in each operation. In short, understanding the Stock Exchange requires knowledge of its rules of engagement. Understanding these rules is the basis upon which all other sound and successful investment practices depend.

"Defining your strategy" involves assessing your personal and financial situation to establish appropriate goals and to design a plan or strategy to achieve them. Factors such as age or expendable income will determine your capacity to take risks and will condition the strategy you should follow to achieve financial goals. You should periodically review your strategy and redefine it if necessary as conditions change. Defining your strategy is therefore a recurring process.

"Picking winning horses" means selecting the best investment options according to your strategy, whether that means picking the most profitable stocks or the highest dividend yields. This involves a thorough preliminary study of every possible option and requires technical skills. You need to continuously review your investment portfolio to assess whether you still have the most suitable options or changes are required.

Lastly, but perhaps most importantly, it is essential for investors to become adept at "managing risks." While careful investors will hedge their bets by conducting advanced and professional studies of investment opportunities, all investment entails inherent uncertainty and no one can be 100% sure that any one investment will turn out well and meet expectations. For this reason, a good investor watches his back against a possible failure, whatever the cause. Risk management must always be present to avoid overexposure to the vagaries of fate. Basic practices, such as "not putting all your eggs in one basket," will save you money and heartache.

In conclusion, these four pillars define a clear process map for achieving success in the Stock Exchange:

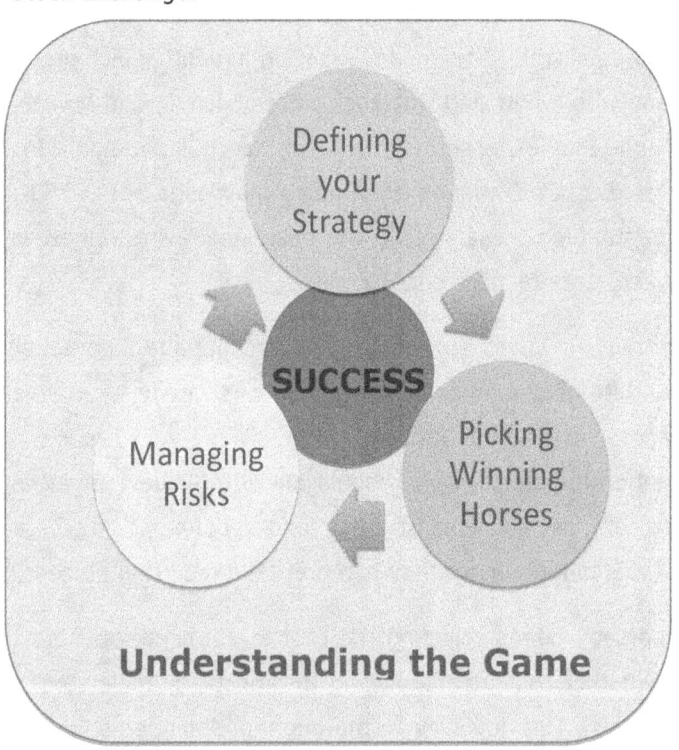

Understanding the Game

If you want to win big on the stock market, you have to know what you are facing and the rules of the game before walking onto the playing field. In this chapter you will learn how the Stock Exchange works and how you can make money in it.

How the Stock Exchange Works

Let's imagine you own a profitable company: it works well and has recorded a sizeable profit every year, but one day you and your associates decide to expand it, perhaps to enter into new markets or new countries. You will need to hire staff, open new offices, purchase equipment, rent warehouses, and more. In the end, you need MONEY.

If the amount of money needed is small, you could borrow it from a relative, a friend or a bank. But what if you need so much money that you cannot gather together enough potential moneylenders? What if the interest to be paid is too high? Then you still have a choice: you can choose to increase the capital of your company.

A capital increase can be achieved by issuing shares of the company; these new shares can be directly acquired by the partners of the firm (and each will bring more capital into the company but their stake will remain the same) or sold to the general public on the stock market (new members are admitted in the company ownership). The money the buyer has paid for his stocks becomes part of the share capital of the company and can be used to undertake new projects. When the investor decides to divest the shares and recover his money, he will go to the Stock Exchange to find a new buyer for his shares.

The Stock Exchange is therefore the place that puts stock sellers and buyers in contact. Its functions are mainly three:

- Channelling savings into productive investment: The Stock Exchange facilitates contact between investors and firms to allow their funding, which represents a vital role in economic development.

- Providing liquidity to the market: The Stock Exchange allows an investor to invest and divest his money quickly, which in turn allows companies to get funded quickly. Imagine that you invested money in shares of a company and suddenly, because of an unforeseen shortfall in funds, you need the money urgently. Without the Stock Exchange it would take days, weeks or even months to find a buyer. An experience like this would cause you to think twice before buying shares of any company, which would slow the market even further.

- Providing security to operations and investors: Every stock market is regulated by a government organization (the U.S. Securities and Exchange Commission, or the SEC, is the regulating body in the United States). The aim of these organizations is to ensure market transparency, correct price valuation, and the protection of investors from fraud.

In addition, the Stock Exchange provides investors with transparency by publishing accurate information about listed companies, and offers small investors access to the capital of large companies. These are just a few among many other benefits.

Although we have been discussing shares, other financial products are also traded in the Stock Exchange, such as government bonds, corporate bonds, Exchange-Traded Funds (ETFs), warrants, investment funds, options, and more.

Why Should You Invest?

Have you ever asked your grandparents how much they paid for their house, or asked your parents how much a ticket to the movies cost when they were teenagers? Sure, their responses may seem ridiculous. Why are we paying way more for everything? Just blame it on inflation!

The cost of goods and services increases each year. Last year, gasoline cost $1.20 a liter while this year it costs $1.25; a pound of potatoes is more expensive this year than the previous one; and surely a beach-view apartment will be worth more in a couple of years than now (although we have finally learned that the price of real estate can also drop). This general increase in prices is called inflation and it is essential to protect yourself from its effects.

Suppose we have $1,000 saved and, as we do not immediately need it, we store it under our mattress. At the same time, assume that prices will rise by 3% and 4% for the next 2 years, respectively. In total, prices will have risen by 7% in 2 years. In other words, we will need 7% more money, or $1,070, to buy the same things. So we just lost money for nothing! To avoid losing money when we want to save it, we must protect our savings from inflation, so that we can make purchases at today's prices in the future.

This devaluation effect also impacts companies, and not just their money but also their buildings, machinery, etc. As a result, they are forced to earn enough money to reinvest in the company so that its value is not affected by inflation. If a company does this, its shares will be revalued proportionately, thereby surpassing inflation. The money we have invested is finally protected.

Protect yourself from the effects of inflation and your savings will not lose value.

What to Buy and What to Sell?

There are plenty of financial products on sale and although this book focuses on the shares of listed companies, the following is a summary of the most common products traded on the Stock Exchange:

- **Securities**:
  - o **Debt or Fixed-Income Securities** are issued by public institutions or enterprises to obtain financing. By purchasing these securities the investor is lending money under the commitment that it will be returned within a specified period and compensated with some

agreed interest. Fixed-income securities therefore guarantee profitability and investment return (as long as the borrower does not declare bankruptcy), although there is great speculation with these products, and you can lose money by purchasing them when governments/companies are doing wrong and offer high interest rates, and selling them at a higher nominal price when things get better and interest rates are low. Examples of debt or fixed-income securities include:

- Government Bonds (treasury bills, municipal bonds)
- Investment Grade Bonds
- High-Yield
- Preferred Stock
- Pensions

o **Equity Securities** are portions of capital (in the case of shares, a company), and do not guarantee either profitability or investment return. By purchasing these products, the buyer is co-owner of the capital and assumes the entailed risks. You can also invest in professionally managed funds to let a professional collect the money and aggregate it with other investors' capital to make the best portfolio according to his best judgment. Examples of equity securities include:

- Shares
- Subscription rights
- Investment Funds
- Mutual Funds

- **Derivatives:**
  o **Exchange-traded derivatives** are products whose value is based on the price of another asset (usually known as underlying asset) that can be almost anything: stocks, indexes, commodities, interest rates, etc. For example, a future on gold is a contract by which the buyer acquires the right of purchasing from the seller certain amount

of gold in the future at today's price (depends on the public price of gold). They are privately and bilaterally negotiated between the issuer of the product and the buyer, and they are purely speculative and typically involve a very high risk. Examples of exchange-traded derivatives include:

- Futures and options
- Warrants
- CFDs

○ **Over-the-counter (off-exchange) derivatives** are the same as their exchange-traded counterparts, but traded in markets where there is no supervisory body such as the SEC (they do not go through an exchange), so they are less safe for investors. These are products with ultra-high risk. Examples include:

- Forwards
- Swaps.

- **Others:**
  ○ Term deposits
  ○ Foreign Currency Accounts
  ○ Pension plans/trusts

In general, fixed-income securities are safer and commonly used for low-risk portfolios; equity securities involve higher risk since neither the profitability nor return of the invested capital are guaranteed; and, finally, derivatives are high-risk and totally speculative products, and are not recommended at all unless you are experienced in and deeply knowledgeable about derivatives, especially at high leverage ratios (the ratio of the investment made on hire, i.e. with borrowed money).

Before returning to the subject of shares, with which this book is primarily concerned, the following is a brief explanation of the most widely used derivatives, as they are a fashionable topic in stock market investment today. Remember that they are speculative products entailing high risk and are never recommended for beginners or to operate long term:

- **Futures** are bilateral contracts (usually between you and your broker) by which you acquire an obligation to buy/sell an underlying asset (stocks, commodities, currencies, etc) on a future date while preserving today's conditions. Imagine that an ounce of gold is currently traded at $1,000, and you think it will go down in the coming months. You could buy a future to sell 10 ounces of gold at $1,000 within 3 months, and the buyer will charge you $15 commission to give you such a right (called a premium). For example, if on the deadline the ounce costs $990, you will sell your 10 ounces at $1,000 to earn $10 per ounce, or a total of $100 (less the $15 commission). The good and bad news for these products is leverage: to buy this future you will not need to pay out the $10,000 worth of 10 ounces of gold but only a security deposit which may be around 10% of its total worth, but you are assuming a risk of $10,000. Therefore, you can multiply your profit by 10 but also risk multiplying your loss by the same amount. You can still speculate by selling the future before the end of the term (in fact, this is common because nobody wants, for example, to execute a purchase of 100 barrels of Oklahoma's oil—let's see how they would get them home!). Imagine that after one month the ounce of gold goes down to $995 and seems to be trending downwards. At this point, some people will be willing to pay $1,005 for your future since it will let them sell it for $1,000 after 2 months when the price has gone even lower.

- **Options** are the same as futures, but you are not obligated to buy/sell the underlying asset after the deadline; instead, you get the right of executing the purchase/sale at your convenience. Purchase options are called "calls" and sale options are called "puts." If you got a *call* and the underlying asset was depreciated then you can decline to buy it after the option deadline, thus only losing the broker fees.

- **Contracts for Differences (CFDs)** are another type of bilateral contract in which a buyer and a seller agree to exchange the difference between the current price of the underlying asset (e.g., stocks, commodities, indexes, currencies, etc.) and its price at the time of contract cancellation. For example, suppose that Coca-Cola shares now trade for $50 and we buy a CFD for 10 shares. If the stock goes up to $55, we can sell the CFD and our broker (the other party of the contract) will pay us the difference ($5 x 10 = $50), but if the shares drop to $45 we will have to pay the difference ($50) to the broker. It is important to understand that this is a leveraged product and the result is continuously updated: in order to buy those 10 Coca-Cola shares you are not required to pay out the $500 but only to deposit a guarantee that may be around 5%, or $25 (leverage is 20), so with $25 you are speculating a volume of $500 and a difference of 1% in the shares of Coca-Cola is a 20% difference in our CFD (gain, loss and risk are finally multiplied by 20!). Note that losses are updated every day in your account (price differences are deducted or added to your account whether they are negative or positive, respectively) and it may be possible that you do not have enough money in the account to cover the guarantees for the opened CFDs. In this case, the broker will automatically sell them and (at that time you are losing big money!). Be very careful with these situations.

- **Exchange Traded Funds (ETFs)** are investment funds whose shares are traded in the Stock Exchange. ETF's are formed by a fixed portfolio of debt and/or equity securities, so their success does not depend on the good work of the fund manager, and they have much lower costs than traditional investment funds. They frequently attempt to replicate a stock index (e.g., ETF Ibex-35 is composed of Spanish shares as the Ibex-35 index, so its ups and downs will be the same).

As already said, the remainder of this book will focus on shares. Before starting, it is very important to know what we are buying. When we acquire shares of Microsoft, for example, we become co-owners of the company, which would become clear when we receive the invitation to participate in Microsoft's shareholders' meetings.

That said, would you participate in a company simply because the share price is high and the company is fashionable? Or would you want to know the development of its sector, its new projects, how the business is being managed, and its performance in recent years?

Do not buy shares just because the company name sounds appealing or because the company is in style. Instead, take the time to perform a proper analysis— you are about to become an entrepreneur!

Stock Indices

It is worth making a special mention of stock indices, as they are often in the news. Stock indices show the average value of a stock market section and are used to analyze global markets and to set market references. For example, in order to assess the performance of the American stock market, we can simply take a look at the S&P 500 or Dow Jones indices.

The value of the index is measured in points and is calculated using a more or less complex formula, exclusive to each index. For investors new to the Stock Exchange, the most important thing to know about indices is to compare the index value of a stock to its past value in order to identify its trend. Indices are not directly bought/sold since they are not assets but market references; however, there are many kinds of derivatives based on them as underlying assets (e.g., there are futures on the S&P 500 index and each point is valued at $250).

There are plenty of indices that represent market sectors, whole markets, or specific geographies. Some of the most important are:

- **Dow Jones**: Originally known as Dow Jones Industrial Average (DJIA), this index is the first in history and was created by Charles Dow and Edward Jones to represent the American industrial sector. Currently, it is

your estimate with its market price. Buy shares when the market price is lower than your valuation.

In theory, the stock market is efficient, which is to say that the prices quoted should reflect all available information by conforming rapidly and completely to supply and demand. Unfortunately, in the short and medium term, this does not happen: prices will lurch chaotically from one place to another for no apparent reason. However, in the long term, in general, the market tends to be more or less efficient.

Therefore, getting into the game of short-term trading is like stepping into a raging river: your exit route is uncertain and the only way to succeed is through careful control of risks and probabilities, plus a certain amount of luck. However, if we detect an inefficiency in the market, such as a share quote price lower than it should be, we can buy hoping that eventually the market will rule in favor of us by adjusting the share quote price to a fair value. Simple, right? So let's find the right price!

A Negative-Sum Game

The Stock Exchange is a negative-sum game, which means that probabilities are against us from the outset: in effect, we start the game by losing money. How? Just by paying fees to our broker and by suffering delays in the execution of our purchase/sale orders.

Each time you purchase shares or any other financial product, you have to pay a commission to the Stock Exchange and another commission to our broker, and the same process happens when you sell. Broker fees vary greatly depending on the broker and the trade value, and have both fixed and variable components. Just to give you a reference, a fixed fee ranges from approximately $5 to $15, and the variable is around 0.05%-0.25%, depending on the amount of money involved in the operation (the higher the investment, the lower the fees). The total amount of these fees (which must be multiplied by two since they are paid when purchasing and selling) can mean a significant percentage of your investment.

Some brokers charge you additional fees for account management, stocks custody, and dividends pay-out reception, so you must carefully select your broker to avoid these fees as much as possible (see chapter: *6 Tips for Choosing A Broker*).

Moreover, between the request for your broker to conduct a buy/sale transaction and the moment when it is effectively executed, the share's quote price may change. This is not critical if you are investing for the long-term, but it may mean big losses for very short-term, or intra-day, transactions.

In either case—in both short and long-term transactions—we are assuming a loss at the very moment we get into the "game," and probabilities are unbalanced against us.

Carefully check your broker commissions and assume them as losses from the start.

Defining Your Strategy

Not everyone has the same interests, investment capacity, or the same risk tolerance, but everyone has to assess his personal situation and adopt an investment strategy that suits his needs and abilities. In this chapter, we will identify the main factors to consider when defining your investment strategy.

Do You Invest or Speculate?

Some people say that investing involves engaging with your assets while speculation involves evading any responsibility and pursuing quick profit. So buying shares of a company and participating in the shareholders' board would be investing; conversely, trading with foreign currency futures would clearly be speculating.

Others relate both terms to the period of time you own the shares. That is, if you keep the shares over a long period of time, you would be investing, but if you sell them in the short-term, then you would be speculating. Thus, buying Google shares and selling them at a higher price in 4 years' time would be an investment, while selling within a couple of weeks would be speculating.

The speculator seeks to make quick and easy money by executing many (and risky) transactions, taking great profit from those going well but also assuming important losses from those failed.

The investor, however, makes few, well-studied, and safer operations, looking for moderate returns but with less chance of failure.

When deciding whether to invest or speculate, then, the first thing you should ask yourself is: what do I intend to achieve? Do you want to make money quickly by running high risks, or do you want to obtain steady-but-moderate returns by performing safe investments?

The second question to consider is: do I have a speculator or an investor profile? Not everyone is able to overcome the dizzying emotions of speculation without falling into an obsession that can cost you all of your money. A speculator has to assume large losses in short periods of time without despair or without attempting to quickly recover by making hasty purchases. A speculator also has to keep calm when investments rise and fall rapidly. In short, speculation involves a lot of stress and the capacity for high risks. Investing treads on firmer ground but makes moderate gains.

Derivatives are products more suitable for speculators due to their lower fees. By leveraging (purchasing/selling on credit, i.e. with borrowed money), speculators can also multiply their potential profit, though also their potential loss. Investors should invest in equities and bonds to reach their goals.

Investing Capacity

When you invest in the stock market you have to start thinking in percentages instead of absolute values. For example, regardless of the amount of money you invest, you should hope to make a profit of 4% or 8%. However, a portion of the fees we pay to buy/sell shares is fixed, which means that if we start with less money we will have a higher initial hurdle to overcome, making it more difficult to profit.

Let's assume that total purchase fees are $8 (fixed) plus 0.5% (variable) of the purchase value. If you invest $100, you will additionally pay $8.50 in fees, which amounts to 8.5% of the shares purchased, but if you invest $1,000, you will pay fees for $13, which is only 1.3%! When we take into account sales commissions (usually an equal amount), you will face a total commission of 17% and 2.6% respectively, which points to the minimum return you should expect from your investment.

Be careful, however. Many people claim that they did not invest enough money as an excuse for failed investments. Regardless of the amount of money you invest—even if it is millions—a losing strategy will only bring you losses. Be aware of the obstacles you face.

Investing capacity refers to the amount of money that a person can invest, or the money that he owns and does not need in the short-term, and whose complete loss would not mean a financial catastrophe.

In conclusion, evaluate your investing capacity to identify the minimum return required to achieve profitability from your investments.

Time Will Tell

Stock quotes usually undergo continuous ups and downs, sometimes justified but often not. Today your shares may rise by 2% but slump tomorrow by 5%. Ultimately, though, a general, long-term trend can be discerned that is consistent with the actual situation of the economy or business.

It is essential to be aware that uncertainty is high in the short-term and quotes are often not representative of current conditions. Instead, they may be subject to excessive speculation, market manipulation by "bigwigs," or investor overreaction to news or particular information. In the long run, the curves soften and randomness decreases; everything tends to make sense.

An illustration of the above would be: long-term movements of quotes are like the tides in the ocean, you are more or less sure where current is taking you and how far you will travel. However, if you look in detail, there are waves that constantly come and go; some are large and others almost negligible, and their behavior is quite uncertain.

The investor has to decide whether to follow the waves or the tides, and act accordingly, as appropriate. If you decide to invest in the long-term, note that you can suffer occasional and temporary losses and must keep a cool head and wait, avoiding the temptation to sell, because if your evaluation was correct and your investment was coherent (in the long-term), you would lose money by selling prematurely. As Warren Buffet said, "Unless you can watch your stock holding decline by 50% without becoming panic-stricken, you should not be in the stock market."

Setting a time horizon for your investments and being true to your strategy while being aware of the risks is the best way to ensure a good success rate.

Don't Sweat the Small Stuff

What if you invest in a company and its quote drops right afterwards? You might think it's just a blip, and that the stock will recover in the long term. But what if it keeps dropping, and dropping, and dropping? How long will you wait?

Sometimes the market does not act logically, even in the long-term, and although we have invested in a good company with great potential, its shares may not meet expectations and may drastically drop. It is a good practice to set a limit in order to avoid excessive losses. A "support" is usually set as a limit, but we can also sell when quotes drop by 20%, for example, depending on our strategy.

Statistically, it is not strictly necessary to win more times than you lose in order to end up profiting, but you need to make thousands when you win and not sweat the small stuff when you lose. It's the first rule of trading: quickly stop losses and let profits climb.

Suppose you choose a company at random, without any information at all, and buy shares. What are the chances of it rising above 5% and dropping below 5%? In theory, the odds are the same. So what if your strategy is to sell when the shares drop by 5% or only when they have risen over 5%? In this case, losses will be limited and earnings will be unlimited. With this strategy, you will be making money when the difference between gains and losses exceeds the fees (remember, this is not a zero sum game).

You can limit your losses by conveniently adjusting stop-losses, which are sales orders that you can manage through your broker and execute when stocks fall below the established value. To ensure profit, you can progressively move the stop-loss upwards as prices rise.

Set limits to your losses and let profits follow their own course, and strategically adjust stop-losses to avoid pitting probabilities against yourself.

Picking Winning Horses

It goes without saying that if you do not carefully select stocks, you will have no chance of profiting in the stock market. Choosing the best stocks is like picking the winning horses at the racetrack and requires a great deal of previous study to succeed. In this chapter, we will discuss the three main tools at our disposal for analyzing the Stock Exchange, each of which has its own purpose and benefit:

- **Fundamental Analysis** helps investors choose the cheapest companies in the Stock Exchange
- **Technical Analysis** allows investors to identify the best time for investment
- **Security Analysis** (often considered a part of Fundamental Analysis) relates the market value of a company to its financial results

Fundamental or Technical Analysis?

Before getting into the details of technical and fundamental, analysis you should know the origin and basis of the dispute between advocates of both.

Throughout the history of the Stock Exchange, technical analysts have argued with fundamental analysts over who has the right analytical tool. In theory, and sticking to pure logic, fundamental analysis provides greater objectivity and its foundations are built on a solid economic and financial base. However, in practice, markets are not perfect, and both mechanisms have some validity.

Technical analysis is based on the repetitiveness of human behavior (in this case, on the behaviour of investors), which actually makes some sense, even more so when we realize that technical analysis laws themselves force us to assume that behavioral patterns repeat. Investors faithful to technical analysis arguably believe in the existence of patterns whose repetition is caused by their own behavior. No matter the cause, the reality is that these patterns exist.

Fundamental analysis carefully analyzes the economic and financial numbers available, obtaining a more realistic and objective view of the situation. By comparing the current situation with the past and assessing the economic environment, it allows investors to estimate the future development of a company. Problems with fundamental analysis arise, however, when the market does not behave logically, which tends to occur more frequently in the short and medium terms, due to several factors: speculation, market manipulation, bubbles, investor ignorance, predominance of technical analysts, etc. Moreover, fundamental analysis requires a higher level of financial expertise than technical analysis, so most people opt for the latter.

Because both techniques aim to forecast the future, they are by definition uncertain. What to trust then? In the absence of a crystal ball, the best solution seems to be to adopt a combination of both methods in order to reduce uncertainty: fundamental analysis will tell us where to put our money, and technical analysis will indicate the right time to do so. Speculation prevails in the short and medium terms while investment does in the long-term; therefore, analysis should be more technical for estimations within a short period of time and more fundamental for the long run.

Moreover, it is essential to incorporate good risk management policies into your strategy in order to put risk under control and not overexpose your investments to the inaccuracies of these analysis tools (see chapter: *Managing Risks*).

Fundamental Analysis

Fundamental analysis aims to objectively determine the real value of a company based on its statements, and further adds forecasts to predict how the company will behave in the future. Macroeconomic factors that may affect the results of the company are also studied: trends in the prices of raw materials used (e.g. crude oil for a transport company), foreign exchange quotes, and more.

Fundamental analysis therefore requires some financial knowledge, which causes many people to ignore it and turn to the exclusive use of technical analysis, much to their detriment.

In this chapter, you will learn the foundations of fundamental analysis.

Perspectives of Fundamental Analysis

There are two ways to approach fundamental analysis:

- **Top-Down**: This approach analyzes the macroeconomic environment from a general view to the particularities of a company.
- **Bottom-Up**: This approach happens in reverse order: it starts studying the particular company and finishes by assessing the global economy. This approach is more limited and should only be considered when the macroeconomic environment is very controlled.

Following a Top-Down approach, a fundamental study will proceed in the following order:

1- International analysis: the political environment is evaluated, as well as the macro indicators (interest rates, inflation, exchange rates, etc.), and the phase of the international economic cycle.

2- National analysis: the national political environment will be assessed, as well as macro indicators (GDP, unemployment, interest rates, inflation, amount of debt and its interest, etc.), and the phase of the national economic cycle.

3- Sectorial analysis: once a particular sector is selected (e.g. transport or telecom), it is time to analyze the legal framework, the price of raw materials, and the risks and prospects for the sector.

4- Detailed study of the company: the balance sheet and income statements of a particular company will be finally analyzed as well as its market share, branding power, competitiveness, etc.

The following chapters discuss these analyses in further detail. In all cases, the analyst's experience is critical in order to draw reliable conclusions.

International Analysis

A large number of parameters can be evaluated when considering an international economic environment. Some of the most important are explained below. The importance of these parameters is not (in most cases) their absolute value, but their evolution over a period of time to detect a trend for use in "predicting" the future.

- **Political environment**: a good political environment, full of good trade relations and few conflicts, is essential for international economic development.

- **Interest rates**: interest rates make money borrowing costs. If excessively high, interest rates will negatively affect the economy by undermining consumption and investment; however, very low interest rates encourage borrowing. Average-to-low interest rates present the most interesting situation for the Stock Exchange (0.5%-3% is a good reference).

- **Inflation**: inflation reduces consumption and investment, increases economic uncertainty, and depreciates currency. However, very low inflation affects productivity and can be catastrophic to the economy if it becomes negative (deflation). Ideally, moderate levels of inflation are preferred, or somewhat low levels (1%-3% is an approximate reference).

- **Exchange rates**: currency depreciation in exporting economic zones will encourage foreigners to buy because it is cheaper for them when exchanging their currency. However, importing areas will benefit from having a strong currency to gain purchasing power abroad. Depending on the trade balance of each country and its strategy, it will be better to either have a high or low exchange. For example, China prefers a cheap yuan to attract foreign investment and maximize its exports.

National Analysis

As in the previous analysis, there are many factors to be assessed for a complete national analysis, and the most important thing is to observe their evolution over time. Some of the principal parameters are:

- **Gross Domestic Product (GDP)**: a growing GDP indicates an economic boom.

- **Unemployment rate**: the active population of a country supports the unemployed population, so a high level of employment is essential for healthy development.

- **Debt**: when a country's debt is excessive and/or is paying high interest rates to finance its operations, production is used to settle the debt, not for economic development.

- Other factors to assess, as in international analysis, are the political environment, inflation, interest rates, exchange rate, etc.

Sectorial Analysis

Prior to investing in a transportation company, for example, it is important to analyze the current economic wellness and future expectations of the sector.

Again, diverse and numerous factors can be considered:

- **Legal framework**: laws that facilitate the sector's activity and do not undermine profitability with excessive taxes are vital for the sector.

- **Raw materials**: if a sector is highly dependent on any raw material (the clearest example is the dependence of the transportation sector on oil), it is important to assess its availability, price, etc.

- **Entry barriers**: barriers to entry to a sector (investment required, competition, legislation, etc.) favor companies already in the market.

- **External risks**: external factors such as weather, public investment, etc., can jeopardize the productivity of a sector.

Fundamental Analysis of the Company

Finally, after determining the viability of investing in a particular sector within a particular economic/geographic area, it is time to analyze companies within that sector and area to select those with the cheapest quotes and the best potential for future profit.

General Valuation

The first factor to be evaluated is the non-financial information of the company, by conducting a qualitative analysis of the company's situation. Among others, the following factors should be analyzed:

- **Competition**: the more competitors in the market, the more price adjustment and strategic differentiation required.

- **Market share**: it is desired to cover a great portion of the market to be well positioned in relation to the competitors.

- **Branding**: good brands guarantee sales (for example, Coca-Cola is likely to keep selling all over the world).

- **Diversification**: diversification is essential to reduce exposure to risk and to maintain constant productivity. Diversification is required in products, business areas, geographic/economic zones, suppliers, etc.

- **Customers**: companies with creditworthy and loyal customers who are internationally distributed in different economic sectors are preferable.

- **Suppliers**: a company should have several strong providers, so that the supply is ensured at competitive prices.

Financial Valuation

Financial valuation is a necessary exercise that allows investors to compare different companies and assess whether their stock prices are appropriate, which in turn affords investors with the information they need to make sound investments. Although numbers are not absolute determinants of a company's value, it is useful to compare similar companies and select the "cheapest" one. This is possibly the part of fundamental analysis that requires the greatest economic and financial knowledge, which may be the reason why many people refuse to perform it. However, intelligent investors always conduct financial valuations of companies. Do not fear tackling this analysis because it will allow you to estimate the real value of a company and to put your money where value really is. Only a few simple concepts and methods are required.

Assessing the value of a company is a partially subjective task, so it's possible to question the veracity of existing valuation methods. However, while these methods are not definitive, they do allow investors to reach a good approximation of value and, above all, to compare the value of several companies based on a common methodology, which reduces the bias that subjectivity introduces to the analysis.

The different instruments or valuation methods most widely used are described below:

Balance Sheet

A balance sheet is a document that listed companies published annually and shows their financial condition at a specific moment in time (at fiscal year-end). It can be thought of as a picture of corporate wealth.

The sheet is divided into assets (or rights) and liabilities and owners' equity (or duties). To clarify, think of assets as the money's destinations or end-products, or, to phrase it differently, what the company owns and what it has lent (stocks, real estate, cash, etc.). Liabilities and owners' equity are the source of the money or, in other words, what the company borrows (social capital, bank loans, debts with customers, etc.).

Briefly, and without having to go into further detail, a balance sheet is broken down as follows:

ASSETS	OWNERS' EQUITY & LIABILITIES
Non-current or Fixed Assets: • Real estate • Equipment • Intangible assets • Investments and financial assets	Owners' Equity: • Capital stock • Retained earnings
	Non-current Liabilities: • Long-term debt
Current Assets: • Inventory • Prepaid expenses • Accounts receivable • Cash and equivalents	Current Liabilities: • Accounts Payable • Accrued expenses (e.g. taxes) • Short-term loans

Table: Summarized composition of Balance Sheet

Each company can break down these blocks even further and will generally use confusing names for the assets/liabilities components, but the information exists and is available to everyone.

Fixed assets correspond to non-liquid goods/property that the company owns and uses in the course of business (e.g., land, machinery, buildings, equipment). Current assets correspond to more liquid assets, or assets that can be quickly and easily converted into cash (e.g., inventory, bank accounts, debt from customers).

Non-current liabilities refer to the funds contributed by the owners of the company (in the form of social capital, stock capital, and reserves); while liabilities correspond to debts to banks, suppliers or others, and can be either short-term or long-term.

Working capital is calculated as the difference between current assets and current liabilities, and expresses the company's solvency or ability to meet short-term liabilities. That is usually referred as liquidity.

The book value, a number that will be used in the stock analysis, refers to the owned resources of the company (i.e., owners' equity), or the difference between total assets and liabilities.

Working capital requirements (WCR) are the minimum amount of resources to finance the normal operations of the company, or to keep the business running, and are defined as customer financing, production/purchase of stocks, and minimum cash. It is interesting that WCRs are as low as possible so that not much liquidity is needed. Debts to suppliers (accounts payable) and accrued expenses help fund operations, so the working capital requirements are calculated as:

WCR = Accounts Receivable + Inventory + Minimum Cash Needed – Accounts Payable – Accrued Expenses

NOTE: minimum cash needed is usually considered null or negligent.

Some desirable references are:

- Current assets must be greater than current liabilities, even as much as double.
- Current assets minus Inventory should be roughly equal to liabilities.
- Owners' Equity should be about equal to liabilities.
- Short-term liabilities (short-term debt, usually with high interest rates) must be low.

A way to evaluate a company is by calculating its liquidation value, or the value that the company would liquidate if it were to sell its assets and pay its debts. In practice, it is useful to see the very minimum value of the company since its continuity has some value, and is determined by discounting all liquidation costs from owners' equity, defined as compensations to employees, tax, and other liquidation expenses.

A different way to evaluate the company's value is calculating its substantial value, which is the value of the investment required to set up a similar company. There are 3 ways to calculate it:

- Gross substantial value: overall value of all assets.
- Net substantial value: total assets less current liabilities.
- Reduced gross substantial value: the same as gross substantial value but discounts the value of the non-cost debt (i.e., accounts payable, suppliers)

Profit & Loss Statement (P&L)

Published annually by listed companies, the P&L is a document that collects their revenues and expenses incurred during the fiscal year.

It can be summarized as follows:

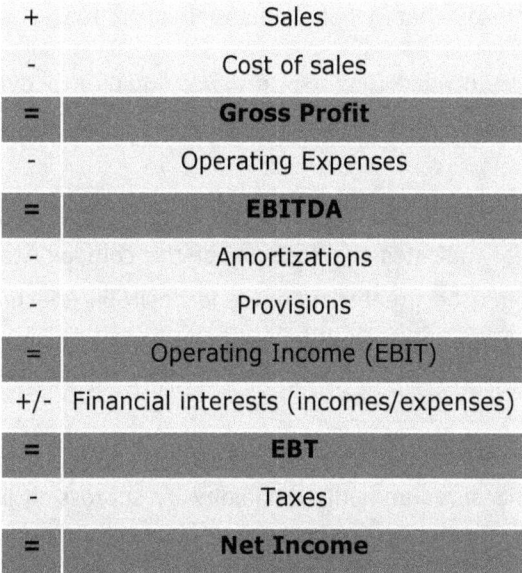

+	Sales
-	Cost of sales
=	**Gross Profit**
-	Operating Expenses
=	**EBITDA**
-	Amortizations
-	Provisions
=	Operating Income (EBIT)
+/-	Financial interests (incomes/expenses)
=	**EBT**
-	Taxes
=	**Net Income**

Table: summarized P&L

The P&L starts with sales revenues from which expenses are then deducted and other incomes are added. Sales volume is therefore the main factor to review, especially its evolution over time.

The second factor to review is the gross profit (which is always positive) and attention should be paid mainly to the percentage it represents over sales, as it will indicate businesses' profitability.

EBITDA discounts fixed business expenses (e.g., personnel, leases, bills) and shows whether the business structure is efficient. This figure is very important because it only involves the normal operations of the company and not external elements such as financing costs and taxes.

Finally, net incomes show net profit gained by the company.

Financial Ratios

A company's balance sheet and P&L statement can be quantitatively analyzed by means of different ratios. Although there are no standard values for these ratios as they depend on each company/sector, their usefulness lies in comparing the ratios of different companies in the same sector and observing their evolution over time in order to estimate what will happen in the future.

These ratios can be divided into four groups: liquidity, activity, solvency, and profitability ratios. Some of the most important are listed below:

1. Liquidity Ratios:

- *Current Ratio*: indicates the capacity of the company to meet short-term payments. Must be greater than 1 and desirably reaching 2, but not too high as a high ratio can mean a waste of assets.

$$Current\ Ratio = \frac{Current\ Assets\ (CA)}{Current\ Liabilities\ (CL)}$$

- *Acid Test*: measures immediate liquidity by supressing inventory from the formula.

$$Acid\ Test = \frac{CA - Inventory}{CL}$$

2. Activity Ratios:

- *Inventory Turnover*: shows the number of times that inventory is converted into cash (sold or used) within a year, so that it indicates how well products are introduced to the market.

$$Inventory\ Turnover = \frac{Cost\ of\ sales}{Inventory}$$

- *Asset Turnover*: indicates the efficiency with which the company profits from its investments (usually calculated for a given year).

$$Asset\ Turnover = \frac{Sales}{Average\ Assets}$$

- *Average Collection Period*: shows (in days) how long it takes the company to collect cash from sales.

$$Average\ Collection\ Period = \frac{Accounts\ receivable}{Sales}x365$$

- *Average Payment Period*: shows (in days) how long it takes the company to make payments to its creditors.

$$Período\ medio\ de\ pago = \frac{Accounts\ payable}{Net\ purchases}x365$$

3. Solvency Ratios:

- *Leverage Ratio (1)*: indicates how much of the company is being externally financed, or the degree of its financial dependence. A high leverage ratio indicates that funding is mainly being sought outside the company and therefore the company has to pay for it. However, external funding is necessary for a company's growth. It is advisable to invest in low-leveraged companies (around 0.5 is a good value for this ratio).

$$Leverage\ Ratio\ (1) = \frac{Total\ Liabilities}{Owners'Equity}$$

- _Leverage Ratio (2)_: another way of measuring leverage is by comparing liabilities with total assets, which indicates how the company has distributed its external funds.

$$Leverage\ Ratio\ (2) = \frac{Total\ Liabilities}{Total\ Assets}$$

- _Autonomy Ratio_: measures the financial independence of a company, which is its capacity to self-fund with owners' equity.

$$Autonomy\ Ratio = \frac{Owners'\ Equity}{Total\ Assets}$$

- _Debt Quality Ratio_: indicates the proportion of short-term debt against total debt. This ratio should be low since short-term debt is more expensive.

$$Debt\ Quality\ Ratio = \frac{Current\ Liabilities}{Total\ Liabilities}$$

4. Profitability Ratios:
- _Operating Margin_: shows the proportion of revenues that mean a net benefit for the company as a result of normal operations, i.e. without considering external factors (financial costs and taxes).

$$Operating\ Margin\ (\%) = \frac{EBIT}{Sales}$$

- _Net Margin_: shows the proportion of revenues that finally mean a net benefit for the company.

$$Net\ Margin = \frac{Net\ Income}{Sales}$$

- _Return on Assets (ROA)_: often referred to as Return on Investment (ROI), indicates the performance of investments or assets.

$$ROA = \frac{Net\ Income}{Total\ assets}$$

- *Return on Equity (ROE)*: indicates the return on owners' equity, which is the benefit for the money invested by the stakeholders.

$$ROE = \frac{Net\ Income}{Owners'Equity}$$

Discounted Cash-Flow (DCF)

DCF is the most commonly used method in modern finance to evaluate enterprises. It considers companies as black boxes that generate incoming and outgoing cash-flows, or, in other words, as entities that receive and pay money.

DCF assessment is based on estimating the cash-flows that the company will generate in the future (through collection of sales, purchase of raw materials, payment of wages, etc.) and discounting them at an appropriate rate according to the risk and volatility of each type of cash-flow to finally get a net present value of such future money. The result is the present investment required to get those estimated cash-flows in the future. Therefore, the heart of the matter is to make a good estimate of future cash-flows and apply the appropriate discount rate.

Let's see a simple example before entering into formulas. Suppose that your neighbor's house will be sold for $200,000 in 10 years' time and he offers to sell it to you right now for just $100,000. Would it be a good idea to buy it or will you be losing money?

To get an answer we can calculate the annual return on that investment:

$$X^{10}100.000 = 200.000 \rightarrow X = 10^{\frac{1}{10}\log\frac{200.000}{100.000}} = 1.072$$

The assessment shows that you will obtain an annual 7.2% profit, which is not too bad. However, if 10-year government bonds (which are supposed to be risk-free) yield 5% every year, is the extra 2.2% worth assuming the risk that purchasing the house entails? In buying the house, you risk the price not evolving as expected and you risk not being to sell the house at that price. Indeed, the higher the risk, the higher the return you must expect from an investment, and in this case, you might require an additional 6% for the risk you are taking. For the investment to be profitable, you have to pay less for the house. But how much exactly? To do this we have to calculate the net present value of future cash-flows, or discount the $200,000 that you will get in 10 years with a discount rate of 11% (5% risk-free investment plus 6% due to the risk assumed):

$$NPV = \frac{200.000}{(1+0{,}11)^{10}} = \$70{,}436.9$$

To conclude, if you could buy the house for $70,436.90 or less, the investment would meet the above-stated conditions.

Generally, for periodical cash-flows (usually yearly), the formula to calculate the net present value of a company using this method is:

$$NPV = \frac{CF_1}{(1+k)^1} + \frac{CF_2}{(1+k)^2} + \frac{CF_3}{(1+k)^3} + ... + \frac{CF_n + RV_n}{(1+k)^n}$$

, where CF_i is the cash-flow generated by the company in period i (usually a year); k is the discount rate or return required by the investors (annual reports can reveal this data or at least provide you with some hints); and RV_n is the residual value of the company after period n (at some point you have to stop counting).

If we consider a cash-flow (CF) and constant yearly growth rate (g) for that cash-flow, the formula simplifies:

$$NPV = \frac{CF}{k-g}$$

The residual value (RV_n) can be calculated by discounting the future cash-flows from a period onward, or simply by considering an infinite length and assuming a constant growth rate (g) for those cash-flows:

$$RV_n = \frac{CF_n(1+g)}{(k-g)}$$

The constant yearly growth rate (g) for a listed company that pays dividends can be calculated as:

$$g\,(\%) = (1 - PayOut) * ROE$$

While several different types of cash-flows can be considered to calculate the value of the company, the most commonly used is the free cash-flow (FCF), which returns the balance available to compensate the shareholders of the company and pay the debt (including interests), or the money generated by the assets of the company from normal operations, after taxes and excluding debt. FCF is calculated from EBIT by adding amortizations (because they are just an accounting entry, not a cash payment) and subtracting taxes and the money reinvested in both new fixed assets and working capital requirements (ΔWCR).

$$FCF = EBIT + Amortizations - Taxes - Reinvetments\ in\ Fixed\ Assets - \Delta WCR$$

The most appropriate discount rate (k) for these cash-flows is the weighted cost of capital (WACC), which is calculated by weighting the cost of the debt (k_d) and the cost of the capital (i.e., owners' equity) (k_e) as follows:

$$WACC = \frac{k_d D(1-t) + k_e E}{D+E}$$

, being k_d the cost of debt (interests); ke is the cost of the capital (interest to shareholders); t is the tax rate (corporation tax); D is the value of existing debt in the company; and E is the value of the owners' equity of the company.

Since the discount rate (k) (i.e., return expected by the investors) is very subjective, there is another financially accepted formula for its calculation (beyond the scope of this book): The Capital Asset Pricing Model (CAPM).

Technical Analysis

Technical analysis is a tool to predict future market behavior from past price and volume data. Its rationale is based on Dow Theory, which can be summarized in three main premises (you will widely find 6 but these 3 summarize all of them):

- **Stock markets are responsive**: prices reflect all available information and news.

- **Prices always move within trends**: they can move upwards (a bullish trend), downwards (a bearish trend) or remain within certain limits (a sideways trend).

- **History always repeats itself**: investors' behaviors are repetitive over time and the effect of these predictable behaviors is reflected in stock quotes.

According to these premises, you only need to identify trends and recurring patterns in the evolution of prices to predict the future. The tools used in technical analysis are prices charts, volume, and technical indicators.

The Importance of Volume

Volume indicates the number of stock operations (purchases/sales) executed in one day for a given company. Although it may seem of little relevance, volume reflects and gauges the existing interest among investors (or the demand) for a given company.

According to one of the basic tenets of Dow Theory, volume is a good indicator of market psychology because it tells us what investors think and therefore moves with the trends and confirms trends' validity. Combining volume data with a company's price chart provides us with a powerful predictive tool.

Below, we will see that patterns in a company's trend change and continuation must be confirmed by its volume because volume tells us whether the market is actually interested in the trend or whether it is a mere manipulation by the "bigwigs". For example, if a downtrend is accompanied by a decrease in volume, it means that the trend is no longer interesting for investors and that the market expects it not to last much longer. However, if the price turns and starts going up with a significant increase in volume, then it is clear that investors were waiting for that turnaround and are supporting it, and, as a result, represents a big change that may be worth getting behind.

These examples show that we must pay special attention to volume to ensure the validity of other signals often deemed to be more trustworthy.

Determining whether volume is high or low is not only about analyzing the absolute value of a company and comparing it to others; instead, we must also compare the current volume and its trend to the past average value for this particular company. For example, the volume of Coca-Cola is between 10 and 20 million transactions per day, while the volume of Técnicas Reunidas (a Spanish company) is only about 0.5-1 million. The difference is a matter of orders of magnitude. If the volume of Coca-Cola suddenly rises to 40 million it would be a good time to analyze the situation and to be prepared to take action.

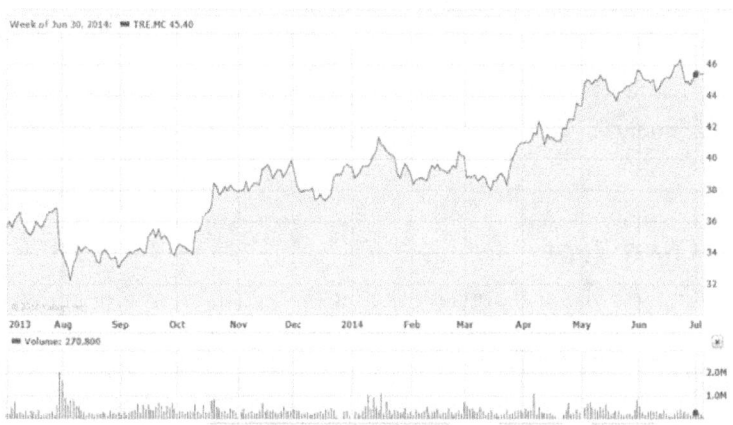

Figure: Técnicas Reunidas monthly chart and volume

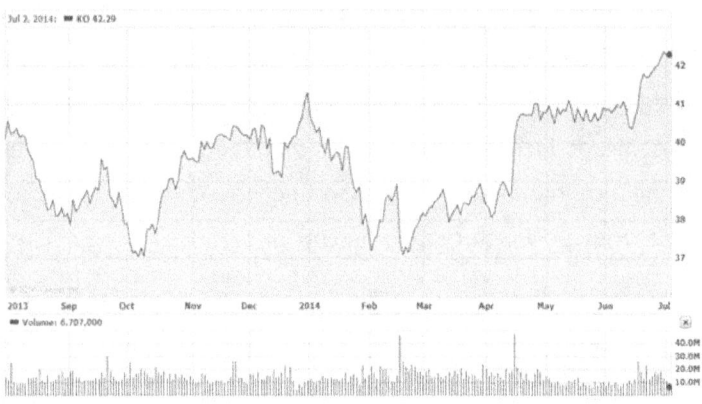

Figure: Coca-Cola monthly chart and volume

Chart Analysis

Chart analysis refers to analyzing securities through price charts only; however, it is usually accompanied by a volume analysis. Price charts represent the evolution of the price of an asset (e.g., stock, bond, currency, gold, etc.) over time. From the graph, we can identify repetitive behaviors and trends, and thus predict what will happen next. Some people exclusively use this information to analyze the market, though this is unadvisable without the support of fundamental analysis.

Pick the Chart Type

A chart is simply a visual representation of the evolution of a price over time (of a stock, bond, currency, commodity, etc.). In the vertical axis, you will always see the price value, and the horizontal axis indicates time. There are different forms of representation, but, in general, all charts contain the same information, which for each time interval includes the opening price (initial), closing price (final), maximum price, and minimum price.

The most commonly used charts are the line chart, the bar chart, and candlestick chart:

- **Line Chart**: Line charts only represent the closing or final price for each time interval, all joined together by a line. This chart is information-poor as it only contains one out of the four possible data.

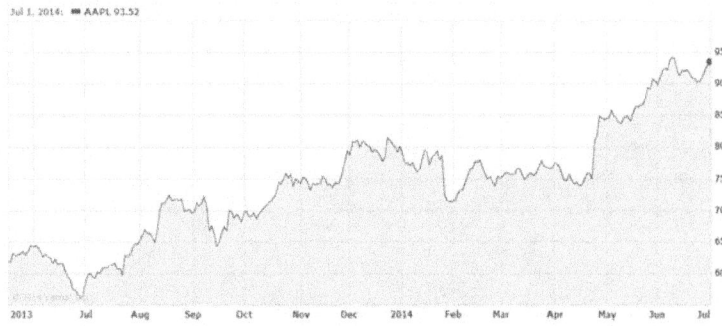

Figure: Daily line chart for Apple stock price

- **Bar Chart**: Also known as Open-High-Low-Close (OHLC), bar charts represent a bar where the lower end is the minimum price, its upper end is the maximum price, the protrusion on the left is the opening price, and the protrusion on the right is the closing price. Each bar is often a blue/green color when the closing price is higher than the opening price (or when the price has increased during the time interval) and is otherwise red (indicating that the price dropped during the time interval). Moreover, each bar can include information for a specific time interval at your choice (an hour, a month, a year, etc.). This graph contains all available information and is very visual due to its color options.

Figure: Daily bar chart for Apple stock price

- **Candlestick Chart**: Candlestick charts follow a similar philosophy to bar charts, but here the opening and closing prices form a rectangle (known as the body of the candlestick). The body will be white when the closing price exceeds the opening price, and black when the opposite occurs. There is a whole science to the interpretation of candlesticks and there are plenty of books and courses that exclusively deal with this matter. In my opinion, this type of scientific analysis strays into fantasy, and I do not recommend pursuing it unless you want to become an avid and nervous trader.

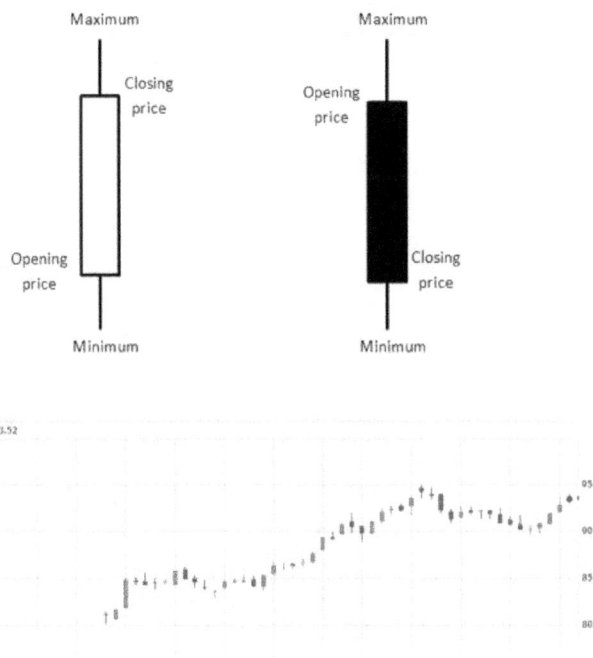

Figure: Daily candlestick chart for Apple stock price

In a candlestick chart, the price axis (or the vertical axis) can be either linear or logarithmically scaled. In linear scales, the axis is divided into equal parts, each representing a fixed amount, for example $1. In logarithmic scales, the vertical axis is divided into parts of different absolute values that represent equivalent relative increases or decreases. For example, an increase from $20 to $30 (50%) would be represented with the same size as an increase from $100 to $150 (also 50%), despite different means ($10 and $50 respectively). Logarithmic scales are useful for assessing relative movements in percentage terms rather than absolute value, but their usage is not very extended.

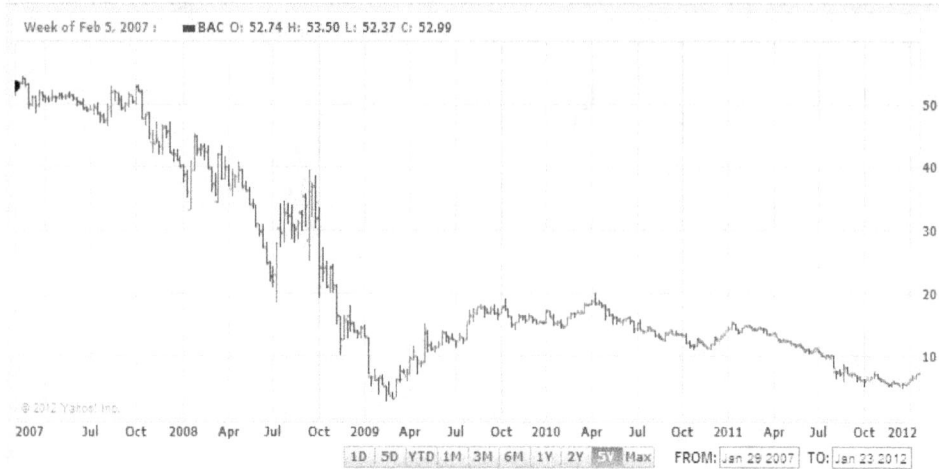

Figure: Linear scale chart

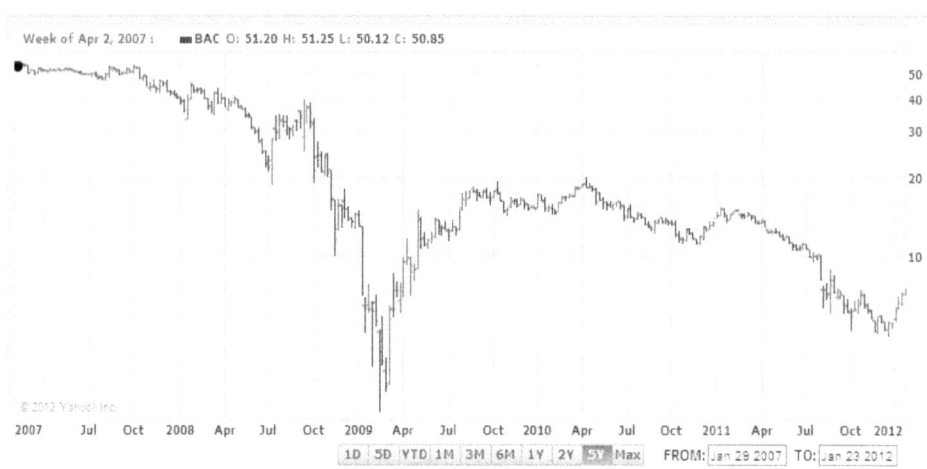

Figure: Logarithmic scale chart

Choosing a chart depends on one's preferences and experience but you must pay special attention to the selection of the time range, or how long the chart will cover, and scale, or whether you will choose daily or monthly charts, for example.

Depending on the type of trader you are, you will want to select a wide or narrow scale. For example, if you are a long-term investor who expects to collect benefits after several years, it makes sense to choose a weekly or even a monthly scale (in a bar chart, each bar would correspond to a week or month) to observe long-term or primary trends. In this case, tracking faster movements in the price over the short-term would only cause confusion. However, if you are an intraday trader expecting to profit in one hour, a scale of minutes is optimal. Choosing a scale of 2, 5, or 10 minutes, for example, facilitates the observation of fast movements (i.e., tertiary trends). In the first case, you will see the price evolution for several years, while in the second case, you will only be interested in what happened during the last few hours.

Know yourself and your strategy and you will clearly understand what type of chart to use and how to configure it. Remember that, in case of doubt or contradiction, long-term charts always rule.

The Mystery of Supports and Resistances

Mysteriously, prices always stop at certain levels, normally coinciding with round numbers. When a stock price is dropping and runs across one of these levels, it hovers there, hesitating, and the quote finally decides either to overtake it or to step back, usually by rising. If the price is going up, the same happens but in the opposite direction.

These levels are called supports and resistances, as they serve as a price floors when quotes drop (supports) or as impassable ceilings when prices rise (resistances). When a price reaches a support/resistance, two things could happen: the price turns and takes the opposite direction, which is the most probable result, or the support/resistance is exceeded, and the price continues its path.

The existence of these levels has its explanation in psychology and in the memory of traders. Let us look at a real-world example, the chart of BNP Paribas.

In March 2009, a clear downtrend in BNP Paribas stock is broken and a bullish period starts from €20. People who have bought shares now realize that they made a wise decision and purchase even more, while new investors get into the new trend, thereby reinforcing it. When the price reaches €60, some investors decide to cash in for the profit and sell. Buyer demand still exists, but the seller demand is strong and does not allow the price to rise beyond €60. Curiously, the price stops up to 4 times around this figure between August 2009 and March 2010. A resistance has just been created and the next time the price gets close to €60, traders will assume that this barrier will never be overcome and will sell in advance, fulfilling their own projections with their own behavior.

Those who did not buy at €20 are repentant and will set that price as the limit to buy in the future. When the price is about €20 again in September 2010, these traders rush to buy, thus suddenly increasing demand and making the price rise. They have just created a support around €20. The next time the price drops to that threshold, "bears" will close their positions and "bulls" will buy, confirming once again the validity of the support.

It is important to highlight that supports and resistances in this example exchanged their role when they are overtaken. In other words, when a resistance is crossed it will act as a support in the future, and vice versa.

Figure: Support and Resistance

The most interesting analysis of this phenomenon of mass psychology that I have read is *Trading for a Living*, by Alexander Elder, which I strongly recommend as a reference on technical analysis that cannot be ignored.

The existence of supports and resistances is incomprehensible to fundamental analysts because they have nothing to do with a company's value and are simply the result of an almost-psychotic speculative behavior. In any case, do not overlook these phenomena because the reality is that they exist, and that we, as investors, bring them into existence with our own behaviors and can take advantage of them.

Supports and resistances are widely studied, and it is possible to **design** trading strategies based exclusively on them, or to use them to support other strategies. The most logical strategy is to buy when the price overtakes a resistance (when a bullish trend is supposed to start) and sell when it drops beyond a support (when a bearish trend is supposed to start), **and to always put a stop-loss in** place and **leave a** margin to cushion against false alarms (e.g., **sell/buy** when price exceeds 5% of a support/resistance).

Stock Market Trends

The easiest and safest way to make money is probably the identification of stock market trends. This means that the work of identifying these trends must be the primary concern of traders. If you are certain that prices will tend to rise, then your strategy is straightforward: buy today and sell when prices have risen.

Any market will always be in one of the following three possible trends:

- **Bullish trend**: prices are constantly rising and reaching new maximum levels.
- **Bearish Trend**: prices are constantly dropping and reaching new minimum levels.
- **Sideways Trend**: prices randomly move up and down within a range delimited by a support and a resistance.

Bullish/bearish trend lines are defined by joining minimums/maximums and also act as support/resistance references.

The following chart for Yahoo! stocks over the course of ten years clearly identifies these trends (bullish (A), bearish (B) and sideways trend (C)).

Figure: Stock Market Trends

As we can see, trends show the mood of investors. If optimism prevails, then the trend is clearly bullish, while if investors look to the future with pessimism, we will face a bearish trend. If there is no consensus between optimists and pessimists, their struggle will be reflected by a sideways trend where both sides exchange power, causing prices to fluctuate between a maximum level (resistance) and a minimum (support).

Although there are different strategies to operate based on trends, the golden rule of trading is to always go in favor of the trend. It is the least risky way to make money and requires minimal effort.

Whatever the strategy, the first step is always to identify the current trend of the stock market.

Strategies with Moving Averages

Market volatility (or speculation) causes prices to constantly rise and drop in a confused, random, and unpredictable way. Sometimes, it can be incredibly difficult to determine whether prices are rising or dropping because of all the "noise".

Moving averages are a very useful speculative resource to eliminate this noise and get a clearer view of reality. Their calculation consists of averaging the closing prices of a number of previous sessions. Thus, the moving average of 50 sessions will be the average closing price of the last 50 days. The average is recalculated for each new session and plotted on the chart together with price, thus giving the sensation of movement.

Do not expect moving averages to anticipate the future. Instead, use them to confirm that a trend exists or that there has been a change in the current trend, always from a retrospective view. This does not mean they are useless at all; rather, moving averages provide investors with important information.

To speculate with moving averages, first select the type of moving average to use and its duration:

- **Type**: we can choose between simple (SMA), exponential (EMA), or weighted (WMA) moving averages, the first two being the most widely used. The SMA is softer because it gives equal importance to all sessions within the calculation range, while the others move more quickly because they give greater weight to recent prices. Because of this, the SMA is commonly used for long-term analyses and EMA for short-term analyses. In any case, for practical purposes, the reading is similar regardless of the chosen moving average.

- **Duration**: the calculation range for the moving average should be chosen according to your strategy. If you operate in the short-term, you should choose short moving averages, from 5 to 20 sessions, for example. For medium-term strategies, you should choose a longer duration, between 50 and 100, for instance. If your horizon is the long-term, then you must choose a long moving average, and the 200-day SMA is very popular in these cases. Note that when I say sessions, I mean any scale selected for the chart (weeks, days, hours, minutes, etc.). Theoretically, the perfect period covers a little more (one more session will be enough) than the distance between two consecutive maximums/minimums.

It is important to note that the interpretation of moving averages and how we react to the information provided to us is independent of the type and duration we have chosen.

The first thing we look at is the location of prices relative to the moving average: above or below. This will tell us which side of the market to be on at all times: if prices move above the moving average, the trend is bullish and so we should be; if prices move below the moving average, the trend is bearish and we should also be bearish. A simple tactic would be to buy shares when prices overtake the moving average and sell when they drop below it. This tactic works well when the trend is very clear and prolonged, whereas in sideways trends, it will generate many false signals that can make us lose a lot of money. The chart below shows the signals generated by the 100-day SMA on the quote of Bank of America over 2 years.

Figure: Buy/Sale signals using simple moving average

When prices approach a popular moving average, traders are on the lookout. Theory says that a trend remains valid as long as reliable signals do not appear indicating the opposite. Assuming this statement is true, it seems smart to act when the price hits a moving average by buying if the trend is bullish or by selling if bearish. In other words, this means betting that the trend will continue and the price will definitely not overtake the moving average. Thanks to this behavior, the public itself ends up converting popular moving averages into support and resistance, so you should follow these averages, though only the most popular, because they move enough volume to significantly influence the stock market. As examples, the 200-day SMA is widely used for the long-term and the 50-day SMA is popular for the mid-term; for the short-term you can use the 10-session or 20-session EMA. In the chart, we can see how well the 200-day SMA worked as support/resistance for the NYSE index between 2002 and 2010.

Figure: Moving average working as support and resistance

Another popular trading technique is to represent two moving averages of different duration and act when the averages cross each other. When the quickest moving average overtakes the slowest one, it will be time to buy, but if the quickest moving average drops below the slowest one, then it will be time to sell. The famous "death cross" occurs when the 50-day EMA crosses the EMA

200 downwards, which apparently does not happen very often and usually precedes a precipitous drop. You can also use three moving averages to reduce false signals. For example, José Luis Cárpatos guides his trading strategy by the "triple death cross" of the 4-session, 8-session, and 40-session EMA (I recommend reading his book "Leones contra Gacelas," only available in Spanish).

The following chart shows crossovers between the 20-day and 40-day EMA for a Coca-Cola quote in 2010.

Figure: Buy/Sale strategy using several moving averages

Continuation and Reversal Patterns

If you look at charts and have enough patience to compare many of them you will realize that there are certain patterns that frequently repeat over time and that the price behavior immediately after is often similar.

There are two types of patterns: those that indicate a turnaround, or the beginning of a trend opposite to the previous one; and those indicating the continuation of the current trend. The meaning of these patterns normally resides in investor psychology, and if you are able to interpret and use them properly you will be able to quickly identify trends.

Usually, these figures are not clearly defined and identifying them requires some imagination, as when a child looks at the clouds and sees dragons and winged horses. This means that the role imagination plays in this process can lead to false signals. However, if we perform the analysis together with volume data we can increase the degree of certainty of the existence of the continuation/reversal pattern.

In this chapter we will see the most important patterns:

Channels

It often happens that in a bullish trend **we** can also join the maximum peaks by a line parallel to the trend line, and vice versa in a bearish trend.

A channel is then formed by two parallel lines between which the price moves, so it is a continuation pattern. Each of the lines is drawn by joining minimum and maximum peaks respectively, and the more minimum/maximum peaks in the lines, the more trustable the channel.

Channels offer good opportunities to speculate in the short-term by buying when the price touches the bottom line and selling when it touches the top line. Furthermore, **they** predict sudden movements when the price overtakes one of the lines, so we must keep a close watch on these events.

Figure: Channel

-59-

Head and Shoulders

Head and shoulders, or SHS (Shoulder-Head-Shoulder), is a very reliable reversal pattern (from bullish to bearish) if confirmed by volume. It is a pattern of three consecutive maximum peaks in which the central peak is highest (the head).

Volume should accompany the pattern by rising as prices rise during the formation of the first two peaks (the **left shoulder** and head) and dropping when prices drop after scoring these maximums, but in the formation of the head, volume should be lower. Finally, volume drops considerably **when the third maximum peak is forming** and greatly increases after this third peak due to the increase of bearish positions.

When the price drops below the neckline (the **joining of the** two minimums that occur on each side of the head) **we** can set a target price: the vertical distance between the neckline and the head, projected downwards. From there, the price is expected to continue falling or to momentarily return to the neckline (a **pull-back** movement) prior to finally dropping.

This whole theory can be equivalently applied to the inverted head and shoulders, a reversal pattern indicating a trend shift from bearish to bullish.

Figure: Head and Shoulders pattern

So it is convenient to quickly sell your shares after the third maximum of the SHS pattern, provided that the volume has confirmed the figure.

Double Top/Bottom

In a bullish trend each maximum peak is higher than the previous one. When this does not happen and a maximum peak only reaches the same level as its predecessor, then buying power, or demand, has weakened and the trend is likely to change. We are facing a double top.

Double tops must also be confirmed by volume: it is considerably lower when price increases towards the second top than for the first top. Once the double top has happened, volume significantly increases due to the high number of short positions.

After the double top, the price will then drop to the downwards projection of the height of the second top, although a pull-back may happen afterwards.

As with SHS, the double top can equivalently happen in reverse order, indicating a trend turnover from bearish to bullish, which is called a double bottom.

Although not a very common pattern, it is very reliable so we must not lose sight of it.

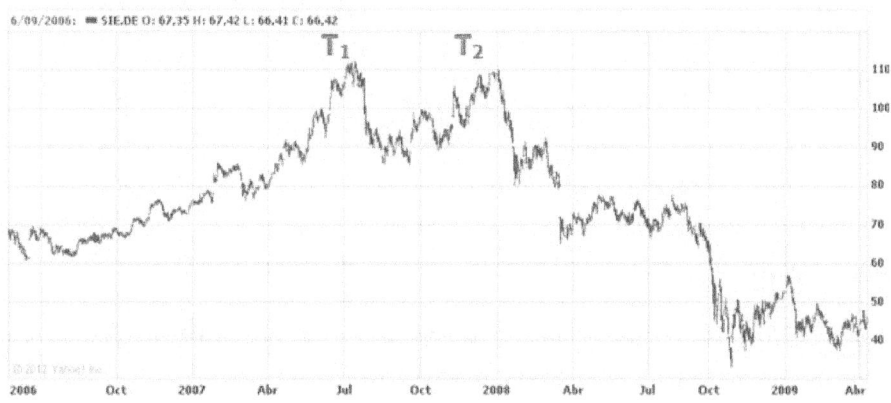

Figure: Double top pattern

Rounded Top/Bottom

Sometimes trends change extremely slowly and gradually; the slope of the original trend decreases until annulled and the opposite trend begins, depicting an arch.

Volume in these cases forms a U: it is high at first but gradually becomes weaker due to uncertainty. When the trend has definitely turned, investors detect it and start operating again, so that the volume grows back.

The longer the rounded top/bottom, the stronger the subsequent reaction.

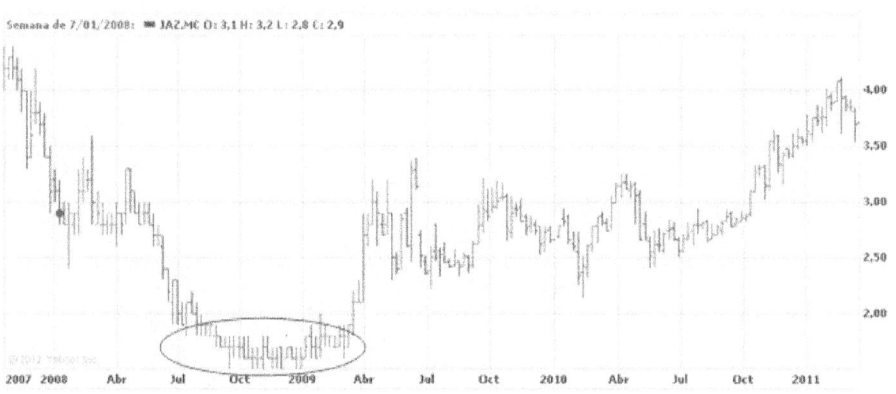

Figure: Rounded bottom

Triangles, Flags, and Pennants

Triangles are continuation patterns, or areas where prices stop to take a breath before continuing on their way. These are areas where prices are bouncing between two converging lines, forming a triangle, until the price finally breaks the upper/lower line (depending on whether the trend is bullish/bearish), and the original trend continues.

When one line is steeper than the other (an asymmetrical triangle), rupture usually occurs in the direction of the steepest line.

Figure: Triangle Pattern

Flags are small channels that occur after a strong increase/decrease to compensate for this sudden movement. They can be either continuation or reversal patterns but, in any case, they commonly resolve in the opposite direction of the flag (i.e., if the flag goes downwards, the price will break upwards and vice versa).

Figure: Continuation Flag

Wedges are very similar patters to triangles with an identical meaning, and so do not require any distinction here.

In all 3 cases, volume tends to drop during the formation of the pattern and sharply rises when the break occurs.

Gaps

Gaps are just blank spaces in the price chart—areas in which the price makes a quick jump instead of moving in a continuous way. It is a price area where no operations occur, which is to say that no one makes any purchases or sales.

Gaps usually occur when important news is published in the time between two sessions, and the opening price is very different from previous closing price. They are more common in illiquid markets, and high volume will tell us to consider the gap.

There are three main types of gaps:

- **Breakaway Gaps**: mean a sharp exit from a congested area, when the market firmly decides to take a direction after time spent hesitating, probably triggered by relevant news. If accompanied by high volume, then the gap is confirmed and initiates a strong trend; otherwise, it can be a false alarm and there are chances that the gap will be filled afterwards (prices return to the area of the gap to reach previous levels).

Figure: Breakaway Gap

- **Runaway/Measuring Gaps**: occur in the middle of a trend, because the enthusiasm of investors grows or new investors join the trend and this new force causes trend acceleration. They usually happen right at the middle of the trend so they are used as an indicator of how far the trend will reach. Again, the gap must be accompanied by high volume.

Figure: Runaway Gap

- **Exhaustion Gaps**: these gaps happen at the end of a trend as a strong final gasp before turning around or entering into a congestion zone for a while. Also must be accompanied by a significant increase in volume.

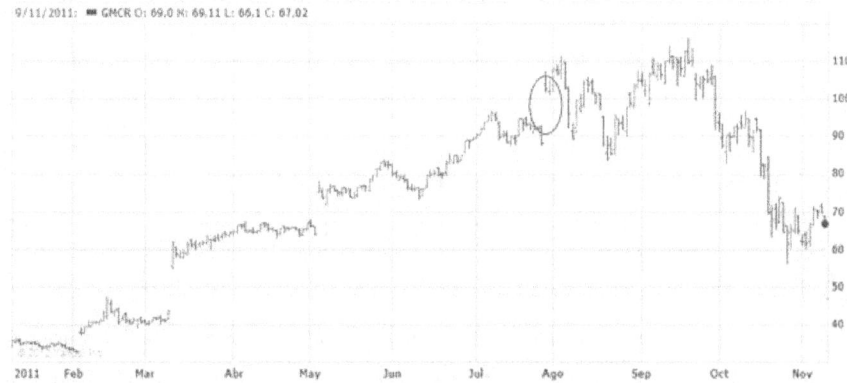

Figure: Exhaustion Gap

-65-

Most gaps are common gaps, probably due to the time difference between stock markets, and are likely to get filled, so beware of false alarms.

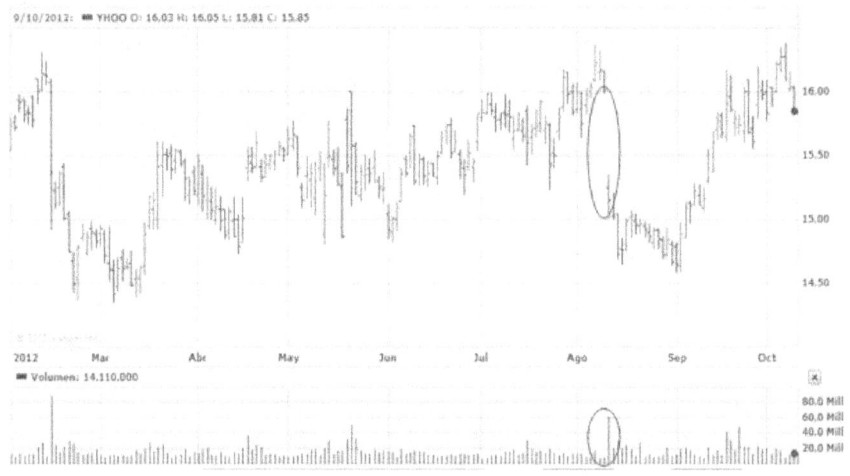

Figure: Filled Gap

Sometimes two gaps may happen in a short period of time, leaving isolated bars in between which form an "island." It is a rare event, but when it happens, a turnaround is very likely to occur next.

Cycles, Waves and Other Esotericisms

If you think technical analysis seems esoteric so far, get ready for what's up next: cycles and waves.

If we take a retrospective view, it is easy to realize that the economy moves in cycles: alternate phases of expansion and recession. After a boom comes a crisis and after a crisis a new boom blasts, and thus the economy is adjusted. Obviously, this affects the stock market even though events occur in advance of market reactions.

If you had plenty of time, a good dose of patience, and some imagination, you could identify a standard repetitive cycle for each market. In this way the famous 18-year, 41-month, and Kondratieff (54-year) cycles were discovered.

The practical utility of cycles is very limited because nobody will systematically buy shares every 41 months or 18 years, but we can draw an important lesson from them: nothing lasts forever.

The greatest exponent of cycles theory is Elliot, who is famous for his waves. Elliot establishes that large bullish markets are composed of eight main waves as in this figure:

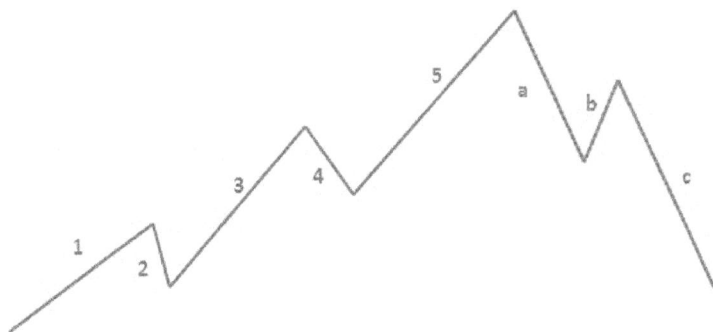

Figure: Elliot Waves

There is a first bullish stage (waves 1-2-3-4-5) and then a bearish stage (waves a-b-c). Waves 1, 3, and 5 are called "thrusts" because they are in favor of the overall trend, while 2 and 4 are corrective, with wave 3 being the largest one of all (never less than wave 1 in any case). Thrusts typically range 1.618 times the previous correction.

Another esoteric theory that deserves a brief mention is the Fibonacci retracements, according to which prices tend to find supports and resistances in their corrections at certain levels (with respect to the previous thrust): 31.2%, 50%, 61.8% (called the "golden ratio"), and 100%. That is, after rising in a bullish move, there will be a decrease, or correction, equivalent to 31.2%, 50%, 61.8%, or 100% of the original climb, before continuing with the trend. All of this may sound absurd and probably is, but the reality is that it works on many occasions, probably because this theory is so widespread that traders are forcing it to happen through their own behavior.

It is a good idea to draw Fibonacci retracement levels on the chart and consider them as potential supports/resistances.

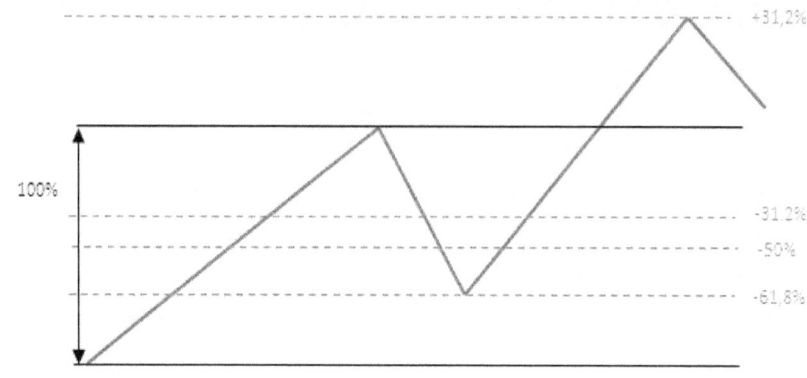

Figure: Fibonacci retracements

Indicators

Indicators are statistical parameters calculated from past price and volume data. They provide information about the state of the stock market and mainly indicate points (prices) for buying and selling, identifying oversold areas (a situation that occurs after an exaggerated descent from which the price is likely to rise), and overbought areas (a situation that occurs after an exaggerated rise from which the price is likely to drop).

Before getting into the matter, note that indicators are secondary tools; the first and most important action to take is to determine the trend and pay attention to certain indicators to better determine where to buy/sell within the trend or to confirm a trend turnover.

Indicators like MACD (Moving Average Convergence-Divergence) or the simple mean indicator aim to identify trend turnovers and are useful when there is a clear trend, either bullish or bearish. There are also other indicators, known as oscillators, such as the RSI (Relative Strength Index) or stochastic indicators, which are used to detect price turnovers within a sideways market. In fact, these are the only reliable indicators in these cases. It is essential to be aware of what type of indicator you are employing in order to identify which cases it can help you analyze.

I only use RSI and MACD but we will explore a few more.

It is important not to rush when facing an overbought/oversold indication, evidence of divergence, or any signal provided by an indicator because these indications show states that may last for a long time or give false alarms. Investors should always wait for the trend to be confirmed by supports/resistances, moving averages, volume, etc.

MACD

Moving Average Convergence-Divergence is a trend-following indicator that serves to identify trends and even points a trend's start and end by comparing two exponential moving averages. The result is then compared with the exponential moving average of the MACD itself, which is called a "signal." Therefore, two lines are shown (sometimes represented as a MACD histogram, but their calculation and meaning are still the same):

$$MACD = EMA(12) - EMA(26)$$

$$Signal = EMA(MACD(9))$$

You can select the length of the moving averages, but 26 and 12 sessions are generally used for line 1, and 9 for line 2. The appearance of the MACD and its signal is as follows:

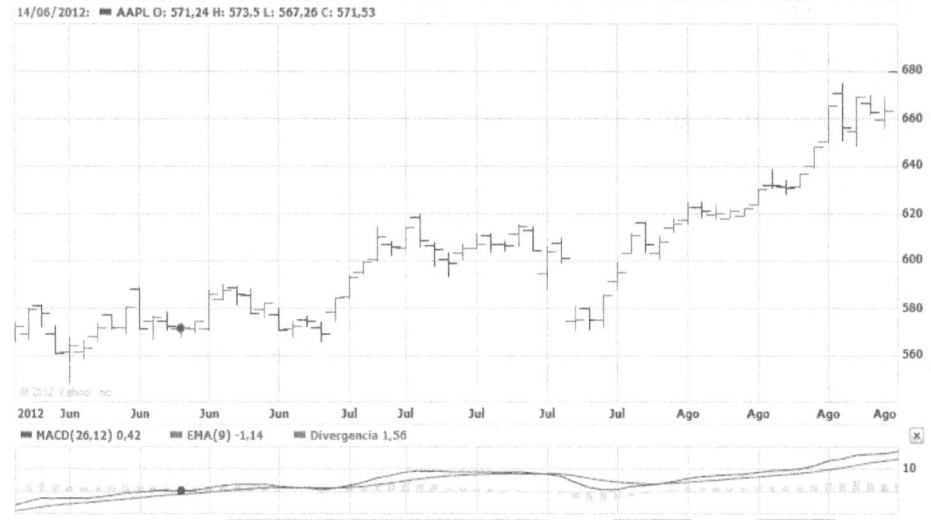

Figure: MACD indicator

If MACD is positive and the fast moving average is greater than the slow average, the trend is likely to be bullish. When, in addition, the MACD is rising, it will be more likely to be right as it means that the difference between the moving averages is growing.

If the MACD is negative, then the trend is likely to be bearish, especially when the MACD is decreasing.

Therefore, when the MACD line crosses the 0-level upwards it will be time to buy; if the cross happens downwards it will indicate that it's time to sell. Sometimes these crossings occur too late (when the trend is already well advanced or even coming to its end) so this strategy is often used in the same way when the MACD crosses the signal line instead of the 0-level.

RSI

Relative Strength Index is an oscillator that represents the "strength" of a quote to detect overbought and oversold states. To do this, it compares bullish against bearish movements in a given period of time, or in the number of days in which the closing price exceeded the previous day's closing price against the number of days that the opposite happened:

$$RSI = 100 - \frac{100}{(1 + RS)}$$

$$RS = \frac{No.\ days\ with\ higher\ closing\ price\ than\ day\ before}{No.\ days\ with\ lower\ closing\ price\ than\ day\ before}$$

The result is a number between 0 and 100, and it is generally accepted that values above 70 indicate overbought areas, while values below 30 show oversold areas.

Therefore, it is probably a good time to sell when the RSI exceeds 70 and to buy when it is lower than 30, always confirming these opportunities with other tools such as volume, supports/resistances breaking, etc. But beware, as an oscillator, RSI is only reliable in sideways markets, when no clear trend is defined.

Figure: RSI

Stochastic

As is the case with RSI, Stochastic is an oscillator whose value is between 0 and 100, but here overbought is defined as being above 80 and oversold is defined as below 20.

Stochastic is obtained from the current price and the maximum and minimum levels achieved in a given period (5 or 20 sessions are typical values) using the following formula:

$$\%K = 100 \: x \: \frac{Current \: Price - Minimum}{Maximum - Minimum}$$

In addition to this line, as happens with the MACD, a moving average (usually of 3 sessions) is depicted to advance the purchase/sale signals, so that %K crossing its average (called %D) upwards will indicate a buy signal, whereas a downward crossing indicates that it's time to sell.

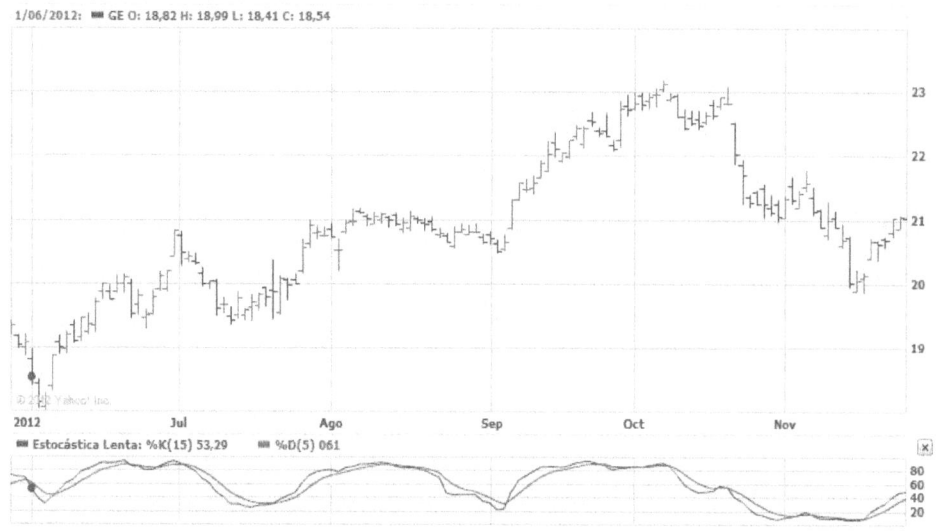

Figure: Stochastic

In sideways trends, sell when the Stochastic is above 70 and buy when it is below 30, though always after confirming the opportunities with other tools.

Momentum

Momentum is a simple subtraction: the last closing price minus that of n sessions ago (usually 5 or 10 sessions are taken), which aims to show the "speed" of prices, or how quickly prices increase or decrease.

$$Momentum = Closing\ Price_{-1} - Closing\ Price_{-n}$$

This oscillator is used to anticipate changes in trend (remember that oscillators work better within sideways trends). Momentum is positive when the current price is higher than that of n sessions ago, and if its value is increasing, it indicates a bullish trend. A negative and dropping momentum indicates that the trend is bearish.

If you decide to use the momentum oscillator, use it as a speculative tool for very short-term trading ranges and when sideways trends clearly dominate.

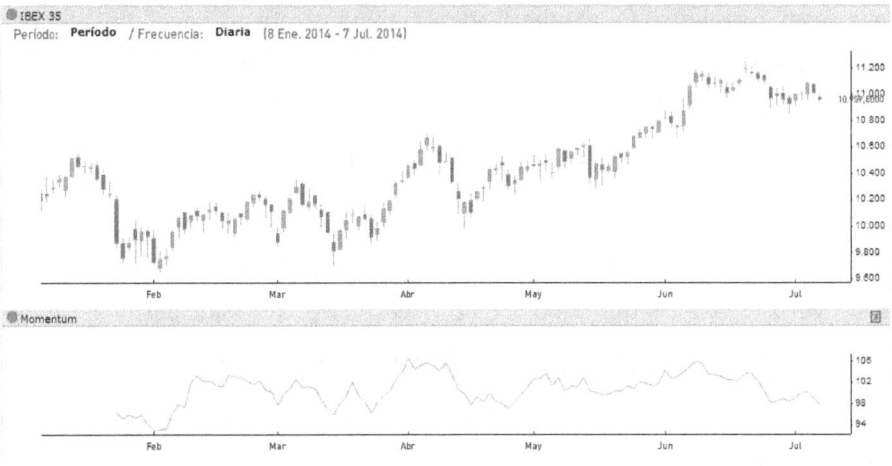

Figure: Momentum

Bollinger Bands

John Bollinger devised an incredibly innovative way to estimate the maximum deviation that quotes can suffer from their average level when the price variation Gaussian-distributed is assumed. Bollinger represented the maximum and minimum deviation by two lines or bands that are dynamically adapted to the new price, obtaining an envelope within which the price must be in normal situations.

Figure: Bollinger Bands

The more stable the price, the narrower the bands, which means less volatility (and usually occurs in sideways markets). In these cases, the price usually ranges from one band to another, so a trading strategy would be to open positions when the price hits one of the bands and close it when it touches the other band. For example, if the price touched the lower band we would buy, and we would not sell until the price had reached the upper band.

However, the best opportunities happen when volatility is high. If after a sideways phase the price takes its trend, bands will widen and the price will clearly overtake one of the bands. In this case, we can take positions in the direction of the overtaken band to be in favor of the new trend.

The most profitable strategy is to bet on price direction when it breaks any of the Bollinger bands, always after confirming the signal with other tools.

Divergences

Despite the previously mentioned strategies, the best strategy for technical indicators is to detect differences against the price. A divergence is an inconsistency between price and an indicator and is usually a reliable sign that the trend is reaching its end.

There are two types of divergences:

- **Bullish Divergence**: occurs when the current trend is bearish, with new minimum peaks happening that are not accompanied by the indicator, so that the minimum peaks of the indicator are increasing. In this case the indicator is warning us of a possible change in trend from bearish to bullish. If we add a line linking the minimum price peaks and another line linking the minimum indicator peaks, we will see something like a "greater than" sign (>).

Figure: Bullish divergence against MACD for Caterpillar chart after 2008 great drop

- **Bearish Divergence**: occurs when the current trend is bullish, with new maximum peaks happening that are not accompanied by the indicator, so that the maximum peaks of the indicator are decreasing. In this case the indicator is warning us of a possible change in trend from bullish to bearish. If we trace a line linking the maximum price peaks and another line linking the maximum indicator peaks, we will see something like a "less than" (<) sign.

Figure: Bearish divergence against RSI for Caterpillar chart right before 2008 great drop

Obviously, divergences are not definite signals but they are quite reliable, especially when they last for a considerable period of time and when a number of maximum/minimum peaks are involved.

The best strategy is to buy after a bullish divergence and to sell after a bearish one, always trying to confirm the trend change with volume, moving average crosses, turnaround patterns, etc.

Security Analysis

Security analysis relates the price of a listed company with its accounts to determine whether the company is being properly valued by the stock market or, by contrast, whether it is undervalued/overvalued. If we detect that a company is being undervalued it will be a good opportunity for us to buy and wait for the market to finally recognize its real value. When we identify an overvaluation, it will then be time to sell.

This identification of overvalue/undervalue situations is achieved by calculating and comparing security ratios. The most useful and well-known are detailed below.

-76-

Market indicators rarely tell much in isolation, but their usefulness lies in comparing values for different companies, preferably within the same business sector.

Earnings per Share (EPS)

EPS indicates how much money the company is making for each of its shares and is obtained by dividing the total net profit of the company by the number of shares outstanding.

Do not forget that when we buy shares we are actually buying a piece of that company. One of the first questions we would ask ourselves before buying a business is: how much money is it making? To evaluate the purchase of a piece of company (shares), we will need to know how much money is generated for that piece of business.

$$EPS = \frac{Net\ Profit}{No.\ Shares\ outstanding}$$

For example, if Apple's EPS is $3, it means that each share of the company is providing annual net profits amounting to $3. This becomes useful when we compare it with the EPS of another listed company or with the share quote itself.

When analyzing several possible companies to invest in, we should give extra points to those with a higher EPS, especially when comparing companies of the same sector.

Price-Earnings Ratio (PER)

PER is obtained by dividing the market price of a share (quote) by the net profit generated per share (EPS), and indicates the market price of the company as a multiple of its benefits.

For example, if the PER of Google is 15 it means that investors are valuing the company at 15 times its earnings. Then, theoretically, it would take 15 years to get our investment returned if we bought shares today and if the company's current annual profit continues over time.

$$PER = \frac{Share\ Price}{EPS}$$

PER is the most known and used security ratio, to the point that many investors base their decisions solely on its value. Clearly, it is worth focusing on, but other factors (explained in previous chapters) must also be evaluated. Moreover, PER usually offers little information in isolation. It becomes valuable when compared to the PER of other companies in the same sector. This type of comparison can be done with any security indicator (e.g., EPS, dividend yield, etc.).

Therefore, we can use the PER as a tool to compare companies within the same sector, favoring the company with the lowest value.

Payout

Payout is the percentage of net profit that a company distributes to its shareholders as dividends. A company with earnings of $40 million in 2012 and a 20% payout has allocated $8 million to its shareholders.

This parameter gives an idea of the company's investing policy. Although there are no benchmarks to assess whether a payout is suitable or not, a growing company will normally reinvest a lot of money (and so will have a low payout), while a solid and well-established company will not make large new investments (and so will have a high payout).

$$Payout = \frac{Dividend\ Yield}{Net\ Profit}$$

Dividend Yield Ratio

Previously, I mentioned that one of the ways to profit in the stock market is through the payment of dividends. Among the parameters to consider when evaluating the purchase of a particular company is the dividend yield ratio, or the percentage representing dividends paid by the company over the value of its share. If a share quotes now at $10 and the company pays out 50 cents per share a year in dividends, this company will have a dividend yield ratio of 5%. This means we can get our investment fully returned in 20 years' time only through dividends, and that without capitalizing the dividends.

$$Dividend\ Yield\ Ratio = \frac{Dividends\ Payout\ (per\ share)}{Share\ Price}$$

When a company yields dividends it is not reinvesting profits in the business so we should not expect the share price to increase too much. Therefore, opting for a high-dividend yield usually means giving up high gains. Typically the blue-chips (large stable companies with low volatility and low need for reinvestment) offer the highest dividends.

You should buy shares with dividend yields in line with your expectations: high-dividend yields if you want your investment progressively returned in cash and lower dividends if you hope to achieve a large profit all at once by selling the shares in the future at a higher price.

Beta

The beta coefficient indicator shows the dependency or correlation of an asset with the market in which it is listed. It is a gauge of the risk of an investment: the higher the risk, the higher the beta (in absolute value). Let's take a closer look at this with an example.

Suppose that Bank of America has a beta of 0.9 with respect to the S&P-500 index. The practical significance of this coefficient is that if the S&P-500 rises by 10%, the Bank of America quote will normally rise by 9% (0.9x10%). Similarly, if the S&P-500 drops by 10% then Bank of America will also drop by 9%.

Now imagine a company with a beta of 1.6. Its shares are more volatile: it will suffer greater fluctuations than the market it belongs to (60% more). The risk of investing in this company is obviously greater.

Cases of negative betas can occur if a quote drops while the market rises and vice versa. This is rare, but it happens.

For the medium and long terms, it is best to invest in securities with low, near-to-zero betas; for short-term speculation, seek out higher betas.

Managing Risks

Even the great Warren Buffet occasionally makes mistakes and some of his investments fail. There is no exact science to determining with certainty whether an investment will succeed. All investments involve risk—risks that we can reduce, but never completely eliminate.

It is therefore essential to introduce a good risk management policy to your investment strategy to avoid completely sinking when things go wrong. The following pages offer some basic rules to strengthen your ability to withstand inevitable failures while still achieving positive results.

The Psychology of Trading

The main risk of any investment is not "out there" in markets or in evil speculators; IT'S IN YOU. Yes, emotions trick us into making impulsive and foolish choices, so it's important that we effectively assess our behaviors and choices, and control our emotions. To profit in the Stock Exchange we must be cold and smart: we must always acting according to our strategy and never get carried away by the anxiety of the moment.

The prices of shares and any other financial assets are constantly moving up and down. Maybe tomorrow you will experience a 5% loss in the price of your shares, but next week they may recover by 20%. Some people are unable to endure the 5% drop; they get nervous and quickly sell too early and end up repeatedly losing money. As Warren Buffet said, "unless you can watch your stock holding decline by 50% without becoming panic-stricken, you should not be in the stock market."

It can also happen that you make a poor investment choice and start losing money from the outset: 3% today, and an additional 10% tomorrow. At this point, there's still time to sell, lose 13%, and simply assume that you were wrong and hope to do better next time. However, it is very normal to obsess and expect a miraculous recovery that may never come, and eventually have to sell with an 80% loss.

These human behaviors can turn winning bets in losing ones, which is why it is so important to define a good strategy according to your situation and personality, and firmly stick to it (see chapter: Defining Your Strategy).

These are some of the most common mistakes to avoid:

- **Excessive pride**: human beings need to show off their triumphs, and investors suffering from excessive pride will tend to quickly sell good shares at small gains and will keep some bad shares in their stock holding just to avoid recognizing their misjudgment.

- **Overconfidence**: when we make money, we get excited, even elated, and we can tend to think that we are invincible. This can cause us to commit the sin of overconfidence and assume higher risks, especially if we are investing with "profited" money, until everything falls apart. When we invest overzealously with profited money, we are like a gambler who, when he beats the house, cannot recognize full ownership of his winnings and so risks them as if they weren't his own, until they vanish. An attitude like this makes it difficult to get away from the casino, or the market, with more money in our pockets.

- **Panic Attack**: if we buy some stocks and their value suddenly drops by 3%, and we panic and automatically sell before losing more money, we are responding to the market without thought or attention to strategy. We must avoid panic attacks by being aware that the stock market continuously moves up and down. It is important to have a clear horizon and not to succumb to the vagaries of the stock market.

- **Blind Love**: it is easy to hold on to a stock that has given good results in the past. For example, if last year we earned good money by investing in Apple, we might "fall in love" and be tempted to repurchase Apple's stock, even if it is not the appropriate moment. We must discard irrational attachments and keep a cool head.

- **Overcompensation**: when a transaction goes wrong and we lose a lot of money, it is easy to feel defeated and to want to show the world that we are winners. This feeling drives us to overcompensate: we will quickly try get our money back by running unnecessary risks. From here it is easy to lose more money and to subsequently feel the need to take on even larger risks, and so on, until we no longer have a penny left in our account. Plans should anticipate occasional losses since all investments involve risk. Be conscious of this and stick to your initial strategy even after a big loss.

The Profit-Risk Relationship

The future performance of an investment is uncertain and will depend on many external factors. This uncertainty is known as risk and will be rewarded with higher profitability as it increases.

Imagine that Real Madrid, a first-division Spanish soccer team, plays against a third division team. What would you expect to happen? Odds are that Real Madrid will win, so betting on this team is less risky. And because the odds are with Real Madrid, bookmakers will offer lower returns to bet on Real Madrid and higher returns in favor of the rival.

Analyze how much risk you can tolerate and select investments that maximize profitability according to that risk; never trust low-risk-but-high-profit products. And always remember that a higher risk investment should produce higher returns.

Young and Bold, Old and Careful

The first thing to ask yourself before investing is: "What kind of investments should I make? Should I focus on buying stocks or bonds or on trading derivatives?"

No clear or objective answer exists to this question because our personal situations are different and we all have different tolerances for different levels of risk. However, from an economic point of view, people in the same age range usually have certain similarities while people of very different ages are often very divergent in their behaviors.

A 25-year-old man has his entire professional life ahead of him, and we can assume that he has no financial liabilities such as a mortgage or children. If he has already started working, his salary would be low but he could expect it to increase over time. If he were to suddenly lose all his money, this young man would have enough time and opportunities to recover.

Conversely, a man in his 60s is on the verge of retirement, and although economic obligations have been settled (he has finished paying his mortgage and his children are independent), he should not expect large revenues. If he was suddenly ruined, he would end up having to endure a terrible retirement from which he could never recover.

The first man, therefore, can (and should) take more risks in search of higher returns; logic says that the second man must protect his savings and run no risks to ensure a comfortable retirement.

If your situation is similar to the first, then primarily invest your savings in stocks, currencies, and derivatives. If it is similar to the second case, then opt for government bonds and fixed deposits. Benjamin Graham, in his book *The Intelligent Investor*, proposes a rule of thumb to distribute your investments based on your age: subtract your age from 100 and you will get the percentage of your portfolio that should be invested in riskier assets like stocks. For example, I am 30 years old, so I should invest 30% of my money in less risky assets, such as bonds, and should invest the remaining 70% in stocks and other riskier products. Periodically review these figures and re-weight them appropriately.

Consider your age when composing your investment portfolio and avoid undesirable situations that cannot be repaired.

Diversify to Win

This rule is simple: do not put all your eggs in one basket. If you ever drop the basket, you would lose everything.

For example, if you invest all your money in Yahoo! stocks and for some reason there is a speculative dot-com bubble that bursts, you will lose most of your savings. However, if you buy shares of various companies from different sectors and countries, you will be able to afford a drop in some quotes while others increase.

You should consider the following tips to make up a well-diversified investment portfolio:

- Invest in companies in **different sectors**: if a sector declines, such as construction, all of your stocks won't drop.

- Invest in companies of **different nationalities**: if the American economy is in crisis then American companies will see their stocks drop. If Germany's economy is strong, German profits can compensate for American losses.

- Invest in companies using **different currencies**: if you have stocks of American, Japanese, and European companies, a decline in the value of the euro will only affect part of your portfolio.

Note that diversification can reduce your profits by compensating good and bad results, but the goal is to reduce risk and, the lower risk, the lower profitability.

Properly diversify and you will reduce the risk of your investments.

Probabilities

It is possible, though highly unlikely, to make money in the stock market without knowing anything about economics, just as it is also possible to win in a casino just by using statistics.

Choose a company at random, without any criteria. How likely is it that its stocks will rise within a certain period of time? What is the likelihood that they will drop? The likelihood of each occurring is exactly the same: fifty-fifty.

So we could develop a statistically winning, long-term strategy only based on this principle. For example, we could invest the same amount of money in 10 random companies that are unrelated to each other (in different sectors, markets, and currencies); when the price of a security drops by 3% then we will automatically sell and assume that loss, but when it rises by 3% we will place a stop-loss ensuring that gain, and move it upwards as the price rises. In this way, we are ensuring that our gains are equal or higher than our losses, guaranteeing either positive or neutral results but never negative. It makes sense, doesn't it?

Of course, to refine this strategy, we should also consider broker commissions, but it provides an example of how you can make money with only the use of probabilities. It is no doubt more effective, however, to conduct fundamental and technical analyses before you invest.

In any case, it is well-worth your time to add some probabilistic logic to your strategy.

Appendix I: Practical analysis of McDonald's stock

McDonald's is the largest fast food restaurant chain in the world, serving 70 million customers each day at its 35,000 restaurants across 119 countries. Originally American and focused on the business of burgers and fries (although it recently expanded its offering with ice creams, salads, sandwiches, etc.), such is its international presence that The Economist has created the "McDonald's index," which compares the price of Big Macs (the flagship product of the company) in each country to provide a benchmark for the cost of living across countries, as well as for the value of local currencies against the USD.

McDonald's is listed in the New York Stock Exchange and belongs to the S&P-500 and Dow Jones indices, and its stocks closed 2013 at $97.03 (+10% in the year), yielding $3.12 dividends per share (3.21% per share), and has been paying dividends out for 38 consecutive years. Currently (November 2014), the stock is quoting at about $96, and there are 990 million shares outstanding, so the company capitalizes at $95,040 million.

We will analyze the company through the data published in its annual reports, including Form 10-K required by the U.S. Securities and Exchange Commission (SEC) of all listed companies and found in the following link:

http://www.aboutmcdonalds.com/content/dam/AboutMcDonalds/Investors/McDs 2013AnnualReport.pdf

NOTE: all data used in this analysis are from the 2013 year-end (latest year report), except for the price of the shares for which the most recent was taken (November 2014).

Fundamental Analysis

McDonald's directly operates fully-owned and franchised restaurants from which it charges fees in concept of image rights, commercial, consulting, advertising, etc. Specifically, 67% of the company's global revenues (a total $28,106 million in 2013) are provided by owned restaurants. Franchisees contribute with the remaining 33%, even though 80% of the restaurants are franchises (profitability is much lower for franchisees but the risk is shared). Franchised revenues come from real estate rental, initial fees, and a percentage of sales.

Geographically, sales come from: the USA (31%), Europe (40%), APMEA (Asia-Pacific, Middle East and Africa) (23%), and other areas account for the remainder (6%). The main markets in Europe are the UK, France, Russia, and Germany (representing 67% of European revenues). Japan, China, and Australia are the greatest contributors from the Asia/Pacific area (representing 54% of APMEA revenues). These seven markets along with the USA and Canada are called the "major markets" and contribute with 75% of revenues. The company's geographical, political, and currency diversification is therefore very good.

Competitors are companies like Burger King, Starbucks, Chipotle, Yum!, or Tim Hortons (recently taken over by Burger King). In general, they are comparatively small businesses in all terms (profit, number of restaurants, and capitalization). For example, Burger King, which is the most like McDonald's, has 13,000 restaurants worldwide and annual revenues of $1,100 million. However, the main competition is Yum!, a group that manages brands such as Pizza Hut, KFC, and Taco Bell, and has similar figures to McDonald's and a significant presence in Asia.

McDonald's has grown in economic terms, albeit moderately, despite the global crisis of recent years (2% annually in recent years, although in some cases, as in 2012, McDonald's net profit decreased), and in 2013, the total number of restaurants increased by 1000. McDonald's also maintains a policy to return to investors all free-cash-flow generated via dividends and share repurchases.

The 2013 balance sheet is summarized as follows (figures rounded and expressed in billions of US dollars, data extracted from the consolidated annual report):

ASSETS	OWNERS' EQUITY & LIABILITIES
Non-current Assets 31,5	Owners' Equity 16
	Non-current Liabilities 20,5
Current Assets 5	Current Liabilities 3,1

The positive working capital of $1.9M (current assets less current liabilities = 5-3.1) enables the company to meet its short-term liabilities. The current ratio CA/CL is 1.61 so the company will have no problems meeting payments in the short term, but the ratio is a little high and may indicate some insignificant waste. In addition, long-term debts are fully covered by fixed assets.

McDonald's Owners' Equity (always positive or the company would be in a technical bankruptcy) represents a high percentage of total liabilities (40%), indicating that the company is solvent and is slightly externally indebted (debt = 23.6/16 = 1.48). Moreover, long-term debt is much higher (6.6 times) than the short-term debt. 60% of assets are financed by outside money (leverage ratio = 23.6/39.6 = 0.596). The book value of the company is $16 billion (the book value of each share would be about $16.20).

Going further into detail, we can calculate the working capital requirements (WCR), which are relatively low and completely covered by the working capital:

WCR = Accounts receivable + Inventory − Accounts payable − Accrued expenses
= 1.3 + 0.12 − 0.22 = $1.2 billions

The consolidated P&L statement (rounded and summarized) is (expressed in billions of US dollars):

+	Revenues	28.11 (100%)
-	Cost of Sales	17.2*
=	Gross Profit	10.9 (38.8%)
-	Operating Expenses	2,14**
=	EBITDA	8.76 (31.1%)
-	Amortizations/others	0.038
-	Provisions	0
=	EBIT	8.73 (31%)
+/-	Financial interests	-0.52
=	EBT	8.2 (29.2%)
-	Taxes	2.62 (32%)
=	Net Income	5.59 (19.9%)

* costs directly associated with both owned and franchised restaurants

** sales, administration, and other costs

EBIT represents 31% of revenues, which apparently is a good figure although a bit low if compared with that of Burger King (45%). In any case, net profit is 20% of revenues for both companies. This indicates that Burger King is more efficient in their operations but McDonald's is better funded, which is a reasonable conclusion as McDonald's is a much larger company (its revenues are about 25 times higher).

However Yum!, a company approximately half the size, has an EBIT of 14% and a net profit of 8% in comparison to total revenues, figures that have been significantly reduced from 2012 indeed; in this case the comparison heavily favors McDonald's.

Expenses are not very broken down, but we can guess that McDonald's has very low overheads and most of the expenses concentrate in restaurants, or in operations, which is a very good sign.

Return on assets (ROA = 5.59/36.5 = 15.3%) indicates that investments are well allocated and profit in a reasonably short period of time (6 years). The equity of shareholders (ROE = 5.59/16 = 35%) provides a very high yield (profitability in 3 years).

Geographically, McDonald's EBIT (Operating Income) is higher in the USA and Europe (where there is higher concentration of owned restaurants) and has only declined in APMEA (-6%) when compared to 2012. The highest sales were achieved in Europe.

ZONE	REVENUES	EBIT	%EBIT	Var.
USA	4.512	3.779	83,7%	+1%
Europe	8.138	3.371	41,4%	+5%
APMEA	5.425	1.480	27,3%	-6%
Others	800	134	16,75%	+46%
TOTAL	28.106	8.764	31,2%	+2%

As for cash, the company had $2.8 billion (US billions, i.e. thousands of millions) at 2013 year end, which is 22% more than in 2012, and cash-flow is therefore positive. The operations contributed with $7.1 billion to the cash-flow throughout the year, of which $3 billion where paid out as dividends. With these data and the low financial interest, we can conclude that cash is not a problem for the company.

Some more interesting information can be obtained from the report:

- The company spent $1,810 billion in treasury stock (purchase of shares of the company from other shareholders).
- Annual growth objectives of the company are: revenues 3-5%, EBIT 6-7%, and ROIIC (return on investment) around 20%.
- The currency exchange had a negative impact on the company's accounts
- 1,400 new restaurants opened in 2013, while around 500 closed down.
- $2.8 billion was reinvested (CapEx), split approximately fifty-fifty between new and existing restaurants.
- 74% of debt is fixed rate so the risk is low, although 41% is in foreign currency so there is high exposure to currency fluctuations (particularly the euro).
- Average interest rate paid on the debt is 3% (0.065% for long-term debt and 5.1% for short-term debt).
- Operations generate as much cash as 50% of total debt.
- The company owns 658 million shares (treasury stock) against a total of 1.648 million (an additional 990 million are free-floating), meaning 40%, a relatively high figure that would reduce the possibility of speculation by large investors and hostile enterprises and would add stability to its stock price.

Let's value the company by means of the Discounted Cash-Flow (DCF) method. Although this method is somewhat subjective and complex, we can still perform simplified calculations to get an idea of the approximate value of the company based on its cash-making ability.

We will estimate future cash-flows for the next four years (2014, 2015, 2016, and 2017) from past free-cash-flow data (in so doing, we are assuming that the company will keep performing the same way). Thus, the net present value (NPV) of the company is calculated from these estimated cash-flows:

$$NPV = \frac{CF_{2014}}{(1+k)^1} + \frac{CF_{2015}}{(1+k)^2} + \frac{CF_{2016}}{(1+k)^3} + \frac{CF_{2017} + VR_{2017}}{(1+k)^4}$$

We could review past annual reports to extract free-cash-flow data for each year, but there is nothing more foolish than to re-work. Some professional websites have already done it for us, for example Ycharts.com (http://ycharts.com/companies/ MCD / free_cash_flow). Here are the FCF data from the past 8 years, according to Ychart:

Year	FCF ($ billions)	Var.
2013	$4,3	+10%
2012	$3,9	-11%
2011	$4,4	+5%
2010	$4,2	+10%
2009	$3,8	+0%
2008	$3,8	+31%
2007	$2,9	+11%
2006	$2,6	-

Average FCF for the last four years is $4.2 billion with an annual incremental trend of 8% since 2006. In addition, after the first two quarters of 2014, the FCF is foreseen to increase in 2014 (improvement at mid-2014 is 14%), which is a great sign. Therefore, we can assume future cash-flow to increase by 8% each year from the $4.2 billion average:

Year	Cash-Flow
2014	4,54

2015	4,89
2016	5,29
2017	5,71

We now have to calculate the discount rate (k) using the WACC formula, knowing that the company pays 3% on average for its debt and considering that investors demand an extra 16% annual profit (3% dividend rate plus 13% on capital gains due to the share price rise, which is the average of the last five years):

$$WACC = \frac{k_d D(1-t) + k_e E}{D+E} = \frac{0,03 * 23,6 * (1-0,32) + 0,16 * 16}{23,6 + 16} = 7,68\%$$

It is also necessary to calculate the residual value of the company at 2017, because we will never calculate the cash-flow from that year to infinity. Assuming a constant long-term growth rate (g) of 3% (this is another great estimate):

$$RV_{2017} = \frac{CF_{2017}(1+g)}{(k-g)} = \frac{5,71 * (1+0,03)}{(0,0768 - 0,03)} = \$125,76 \; billions$$

Finally, the value of the company is:

$$NPV = \frac{CF_{2014}}{(1+k)^1} + \frac{CF_{2015}}{(1+k)^2} + \frac{CF_{2016}}{(1+k)^3} + \frac{CF_{2017} + VR_{2017}}{(1+k)^4} =$$

$$= \frac{4,54}{(1+0,0768)^1} + \frac{4,89}{(1+0,0768)^2} + \frac{5,29}{(1+0,0768)^3} + \frac{5,71 + 125,76}{(1+0,0768)^4} = \$110,46 \; billions$$

Dividing this figure by the number of shares of the company (990 million free-floating), we obtain the theoretical value of the shares: **$111.57**.

You can compare this value with professional assessments such as that by Stock Analysis On Net (http://www.stock-analysis-on.net/NYSE/Company/McDonalds-Corp/DCF/Present-Value-of-FCFF#Intrinsic-Stock-Value), which estimates the value of McDonald's stock at $114.80 and is probably conducted by far more complex and difficult-to-understand calculations, as well as that of www.gurufocus.com, whose estimate is $108.56.

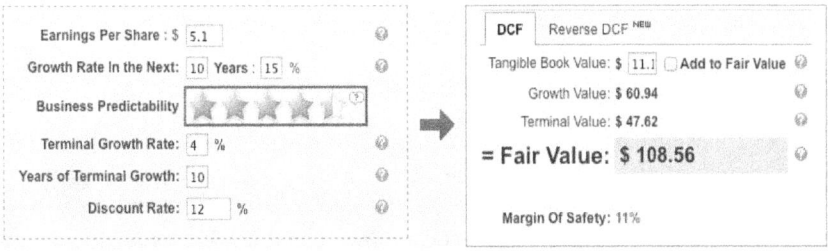

In conclusion, as the company stock now trades at around $96 (November 2014), we could state it is undervalued (with a safety margin of 16.2%). We have identified a buying opportunity.

Technical Analysis

We will now estimate the trend of the stock price in the long-run by means of a monthly chart of 10 years and a simple moving average of 12 months:

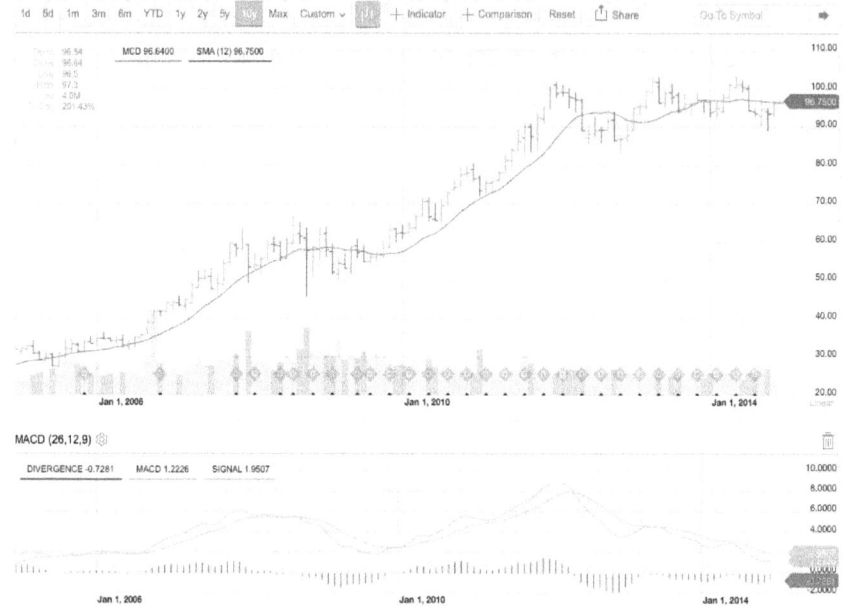

Figure: McDonald's monthly chart

The overall trend has been generally bullish since mid-2011 but is now stalled in an over-long sideways trend, which is apparently a secondary trend. The price is nearly at maximum level and about to cross the simple moving average of 12 months. Furthermore, the MACD indicates that we are in a bearish period, probably coming to an end because the indicator is very low. The volume has remained stable over the last four years.

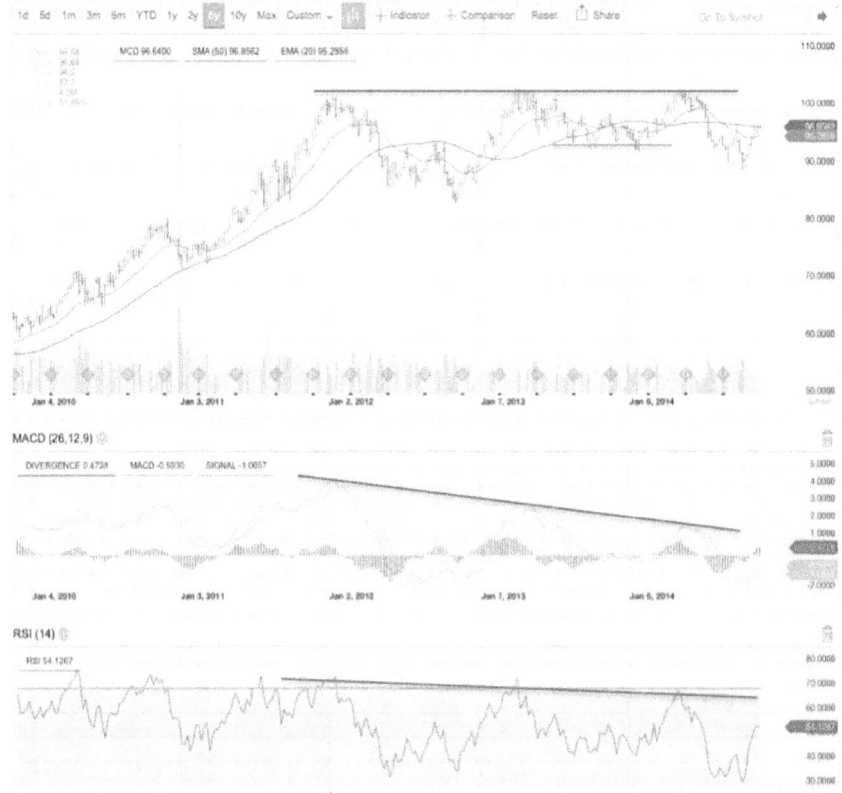

Figure: McDonald's weekly chart

Looking at a mid-term chart, in this case a weekly chart of five-years duration, we can observe this sideways trend more clearly. In this case, within this sideways trend, it may be a good time to buy because the fast MACD line has just crossed the slow line and is about to move to positive values. Moreover, adding an exponential moving average of medium speed (20 weeks), we see that it just turned towards a positive trend. Finally, the RSI is in medium values so this information is not relevant.

This sideways movement is confirmed by observing the divergences between the maximum price peaks that are at the same level (there are 3 maximum peaks at around $103) and the maximum MACD or RSI peaks, which are decreasing, although this signal could be interpreted as a premonition of a turnaround.

Should we buy shares, the short-term objective would be the strong resistance at around $103 and we may set a stop-loss at the $94 resistance (since we would be speculating in the short-term). For long-term investments we should be cautious and wait for price to exceed the $103 resistance. As a final strategy combining these two options, we could buy now and put a stop-loss at $94, and when the price exceeds $103 we could move the stop-loss up to this figure and wait for the price to rise even more.

Figure: McDonald's daily chart

Performing the same analysis on a daily chart covering two years, we confirm previous findings regarding the advisability of buying for the short-term. However, in this case, RSI looks overbought, so we might expect a small correction in the coming days.

Security Analysis

The price to be considered for a security analysis is the latest one, or $96 (remember this analysis is being performed in November 2014). However, the last financial report is for the 2013 year-end and so is somewhat outdated. For a company as stable as McDonald's, this is negligible. The most important ratios are:

$EPS = 5586/990 = \$5.64$ (5.88%)

$PER = 96/5.64 = 17.02$

Capitalization $= 96*990$Mill$= \$95.040$ Millions

Price/book value $= 95.04/16 = 5.94$

As a first-look analysis, the EPS is quite good: the company earns $5.64 per year per share, or 5.88% of the share price. The PER seems low and the share price compared to its book value looks reasonable (about 6 times higher).

In any case, we must compare these values to those of other companies within the same sector to ensure that the analysis is valid and relevant. Results are strong in comparison to Burger King, Yum!, and Starbucks. By far, McDonald's outperforms them all:

	BPA	PER	Price/Book
McDonald's	$5.64 (5.9%)	17.02	5.94
Burger King	$0.87 (2.7%)	38.08	8.43
Yum!	$2.36 (3.1%)	21.85	13.20
Starbucks	$2.65 (3.4%)	30.64	12.25

The company participates in the S&P-500 and Dow Jones indices, with a Beta of 0.62 which means a certain level of independence from the indices and low volatility.

Stock market sentiment tells us what most investors/speculators are doing and can be easily deduced from the "Short Percent of Float" (SPF) parameter, which indicates the percentage of shares short-positioned (yes, you can bet that a stock will drop, and I say "bet" because it is pure speculation) for all the free-float. For McDonald's, the SPF is 1.3% (source: Morningstar quotes), which is similar to that of its competitors (Yum! has an SPF of 1.1%, Starbucks's SPF is 1.3%, and Burger King has a big problem with a 40% SPF). In addition, the put/call ratio (the number of bearish options in the market against bullish options, a parameter that indicates what options traders are making) is less than 1%, so options traders are generally bullish on McDonald's.

Finally, on NASDAQ's website (http://www.nasdaq.com/symbol/mcd/insider-trades), we can check what kind of operations the "insiders" are making (insiders are people from inside the company as executives of the top management) over the last year. In the case of McDonald's, these operations are all sales, which is not good news, as it may mean that company executives are dumping their shares.

As for the composition of shareholders, 65.3% of the "float" is in the hands of institutions and 0.04% is controlled by the "insiders."

Conclusion

McDonald's has powerful branding and holds a position of clear market leadership. Its evolution in terms of growth is steady and consistent, and it is present worldwide.

The fundamental data on McDonald's are downright good, with healthy and balanced statements. The level of indebtedness is appropriate and profitability (EBIT) is high. In addition, the company has the capacity to generate positive cash-flows. The DCF valuation is positive, which is to say that there is a buying opportunity because the shares are being undervalued by the stock market. Share price should be around $111, $15 more than the current price.

The security analysis shows an attractive situation compared to other companies, and presents us with an invitation to buy shares. The low volatility and dividends yield make McDonald's a perfect company for long-term portfolios with little risk. However, technical analysis detected no long-term buying signals at the moment, although there are some for the short-term to speculate within a sideways trend.

Keep in mind that the US dollar is strong against the euro right now (EUR/USD = 1.24), which makes shares more expensive to foreign buyers. This factor is very important when buying stocks listed in a different currency.

To summarize, since the parameters that Warren Buffet focuses on to buy stocks are all positive (branding, low debt, high profitability and the ability to generate cash), McDonald's is a great company to invest in for the long-term, and we can say this almost without hesitation. However, it is not clear that this is the best time to buy as a technical analysis reveals no clear opportunity and you may want to wait for the price of the US dollar to drop if your account is in another currency.

DISCLAIMER: This analysis is subjective. It is in no way an attempt to convince the reader to buy or sell McDonald's stocks, but encourages him/her to conduct his/her own research and make his/her own conclusions. It is presented here as an illustrative example of stock analysis.

Appendix II: Get Ready to Invest

PaperTesting

Before you start investing your hard-earned savings, you must learn as much as possible. Surely this is not the first book you have read about stock analysis, and don't let it be your last. Keep studying, be restless and curious, and above all OBSERVE.

It is essential to thoroughly observe the stock market before getting into it. Notice when prices move, which signals coincide with those movements, how many times an oscillator fails (i.e., how many times it gives false signals), and how many times other indicators are correct. Ask yourself at all times what you would do in the situations you are observing. Would you buy? Would you sell? Or would you wait for a better opportunity?

In other words, practice what I call "papertesting." I take the word "papertesting" from the idea of "papertrading," but since papertrading is associated with speculation, I want to emphasize the word "test" over "trade." Papertesting involves pretending that you are investing without putting real money at risk. It is an absolute must to spend an extended period of time—I recommend a minimum of one year—observing the stock market and making note of how you would act in the scenarios you observe.

Record the date and the reasons that led you to hypothetically buy or sell and then evaluate whether your choices would have been successful or unsuccessful. Many websites allow you to create fictitious portfolios and do this sort of tracking. When you guess right, use the same reasoning in the future; otherwise, evaluate why you failed.

If you find yourself making good hypothetical investments from the get-go, do not be tempted into thinking you are missing opportunities to make money in the stock market. Good guesses at the outset can be a simple coincidence and there will always be opportunities to invest and earn real money in the stock market. They will be there waiting for you. This time spent observing and learning from the market may very well be the best time spent in your life as an investor. And it doesn't have to be boring! Make it a game! Are you winning or losing?

Stock Purchases and Sales in Practice

Purchases and sales of shares or any other product are performed through the trading platform of your broker, via electronic orders. These orders specify how many shares you want to buy/sell, at what price, and when. The main types of orders are:

- **Market Orders**: a specified number of shares are purchased/sold at the current market price.

- **Limit Orders**: a maximum purchase price or minimum sale price is established to perform the operation. For example, if the current quote price is $19.30, you can put a purchase order in to your broker of 40 shares at a maximum price of $19.35, thereby avoiding an eventual increase before the operation is executed.

- **Stop Orders**: the order is only issued when the price reaches a certain price, and then it is set as a market order. For example, if the current quote price is $5.90 and we have identified a resistance at $6.00, we could place an order to buy shares when the stock price exceeds $6.10 (resistance overcome).

- **Stop-Limit Orders**: these are a mix between the two previous orders and are only released when the price reaches a certain level, and then placed as a limited order.

- **Trailing Stop Orders**: when you already own a stock with profit you can specify a percentage of the price value at which you want to sell if the price drops, thereby ensuring some profit. If the price rises, the order will automatically move up, always keeping the percentage specified.

Also, you should consider the duration of orders since you can choose to have them active in the market for only one day (a day order) or for several days (a GTC, or Good 'Till Cancelled order), for up to 3 months.

6 Tips for Choosing A Broker

Nobody directly goes to the Stock Exchange to buy shares, waving his hand and hysterically shouting like you might see in the movies. Everything works in a less glamorous, but more practical, way: from your computer at home through a trading platform. This platform connects you with your broker who acts as a financial intermediary between you and the Stock Exchange by executing your purchase/sale orders.

The broker is therefore your tool for interacting with the market, and as such is an essential element that must be carefully selected.

When choosing your broker:

- Reward those offering the cheapest **commissions** based on your expected activity: brokers are never free and will practically charge you every chargeable penny for every single service (for every purchase, every sale, for cashing dividends, for holding your stocks, just to keep your account active, etc.). It is vital that the fees are reasonable if you do not want your account running to zero before even putting an order in place. There are several types of commissions, and which ones you should focus on when selecting a broker depend on whether you are trading in the long-term or in the short-term. For example, long-term investors should care more about stock holding commissions while short-term traders should focus on finding low purchase/sale commissions.

- Make sure your broker can broker trades in the **markets** you are interested in: what market are you operating in? Spanish stocks, American stocks, currencies trading, derivatives? Your broker should provide you with access to these markets (for reasonable commissions).

- Pay for **stock information** services only if you are using it: many brokers offer customer advice and information on market evolution and news. These so-called full-service brokers are more expensive than discount brokers that do not offer these services. If you would like to work with a broker that can keep you updated on stock market evolution, be sure to investigate the quality and relevance of the information provided. For example, consider questions like: What information can the broker offer and on which markets, and how often is the information updated? Ensure that the cost of these services with respect to a discount broker is acceptable.

- Look at the quality of the **trading platform**: as a trader/investor, you make your purchase/sale orders through software provided by the broker. This platform should be as comfortable and intuitive as possible. It is recommended to first open a trial account to see for yourself which software works for you.

- Check that the broker allows you to place all the types of **stops and orders** that you want to use: there are many types of stops and orders and not all are available at any broker. For example, it may happen that a broker only offers stop-loss orders that expire at the end of the day, which would only be suitable for intraday investors.

- Consider the value of **portfolio tracking** information: whether you keep track of your investment portfolio using a more powerful tool or simply Excel, it can be helpful to obtain data directly from the broker. If this information is available and presented in a clear format, give some extra points to that broker.

In general, it is impossible to say objectively that any one broker is better than another, but an intraday trader who exclusively operates in the American market might prefer a broker that would not be appropriate for a long-term investor who only operates in the Spanish market. In fact, you should have several brokers to operate with several different strategies. Use one for European markets and another for the American market as commissions will be disparate, or one for short-term operations and another for long-term operations.

In any case, before contracting a broker, do thorough research on the internet. Compare rates and services, **ensure your prospective broker can** cover all your needs, **and** read plenty of reviews in forums.

These are some of the most widely recognized brokers:

- TD Ameritrade
- Interactive Brokers
- Scottrade
- TradeKing
- E-Trade
- TradeMonster
- Place Trade
- ING Direct
- Trade Station
- OptionsXpress

Trading Platform

A trading platform is the software through which we generate our purchase/sale orders. Brokers usually offer adequate trading platforms for a regular investor, but if your profile is more professional or **you** do top-flight trading, **then you** may need something more complete that provides other additional features (**e.g.,** **more** types of orders or the possibility of programming automated trading systems).

In that case, you can acquire a trading platform and synchronize it with your broker so that you only use the trading platform **of your choice** and do everything through it.

Some of the most common platforms that you can install are VisualChart, ProRealTime, Metatrader, and NinjaTrader, which access a database and present results on your screen. In general, these programs are free for deferred data (data are delayed by 15 minutes), but charge high fees to get real-time information. VisualChart is undoubtedly the most prestigious but also one of the most expensive, you can see its rates here: http://www.visualchart.com/precio/?it=436&pnl

Again, the average investor does not need any of these platforms and can instead use those provided by a broker.

Sources of Information

Information is the main tool we have at our disposal to make sound investment decisions and can be almost anything from technical indicators to international economic news. In this section, we will review the most reliable and complete sources of investment information.

For fundamental analysis purposes balance sheets and income statements directly published by the company you are analyzing are vital. Both documents are available on the website of the company, usually contained in a document called "Annual Report," which includes other relevant information to the shareholder. This report must be published by all listed companies. For American companies, this report is called a "Form 10-K".

You can also find useful information about listed companies on the websites of commissions: for example, the SEC (www.sec.gov) in the USA or the CNMV (www.cnmv.es) in Spain.

Regarding securities ratios (BPA, PER, etc), there are many financial pages calculating them, so there is no need to do it yourself. For example, visit the financial section of Yahoo!: www.finance.yahoo.com

To perform a technical analysis, www.infobolsa.es and www.finance.yahoo.com offer good editable charts. While brokers' trading platforms may be sufficient, the information provided often leaves much to be desired.

All that said, the most complete website is probably www.morningstar.com. There you can find all of the information you need integrated in one place, such as reports on various industrial sectors or historic dividend **yield** for each company.

Additionally, **it is advisable** to stay up-to-date with the latest economic and financial news. For this you can read on-**line** financial newspapers or follow blogs by experts (**these** also can give you good ideas for your personal investments). Here are my recommendations:

Morningstar	Yahoo!
www.morningstar.es	www.finance.yahoo.com
Financial Times	Guru Focus
www.ft.com	www.gurufocus.com
Finviz	4-traders
www.finviz.com	www.4-traders.com
YCharts	Bloomberg
www.ycharts.com	www.bloomberg.com

Caution: "Experts" Talking!

You can find a surprising number of experts in every subject, and this is no different in stock market analysis. Many expert traders have personal blogs, write in specialized journals or participate on TV shows giving their predictions on the future of the stock market.

Some of them credibly argue their predictions and may ultimately be right or wrong, as anyone trying to anticipate the future would be. But most are fake gurus who earn something when you invest in the securities they recommend—they may have contracts with a broker or just look to increase demand of particular stocks because they have them in their portfolios.

In any case, never trust anyone immediately. It is best to wait and check over multiple cases whether he/she tends to give good recommendations before you decide to rely on him/her. Even seemingly reputable rating agencies (such as Moody's, Standard & Poor's, Fitch, etc.) can be one of these fake experts moved by interest—if you do not believe me, remember that Lehman Brothers' had the highest rating just before it went bankrupt.

In general, it is not a bad idea to do the opposite of what the media says as they always begin to preach stock market booms or bubbles after exaggerated rises and just before they explode and dramatically drop. Conversely, when prices have dropped too much and there are good opportunities to buy, everyone talks about how bad the situation is, spreading pessimism and making things worse, but this is the best time to buy. This strategy is known as "contrarian investing," or doing the opposite of what the crowd says, and it actually works in many cases.

Recommended Reading List

Bookstores carry plenty of publications on speculation and investment—some are quite useful while others only offer piecemeal advice that won't help you develop a strong investment strategy. Regardless, it is highly recommended that prospective investors read voraciously on the subject, while maintaining a critical eye and only picking what is helpful for their unique profile as an investor/trader.

The books I cite here are the ones that helped me learn the most about the stock market; these are books with practical information written by professionals. In order, these are my recommendations for further learning:

The Intelligent Investor (Benjamin Graham)

May be the best book ever written about long-term value investing, which Warren Buffet has always followed with obvious success. It is a book for all ages in which the author sensibly argues his views on investment and market behavior. Although a little outdated (especially the examples), Graham's investment philosophy is still perfectly applicable.

Trading for a Living (Alexander Elder)

A fairly comprehensive book on psychological trading. The psychiatrist Alexander Elder aptly sums up the world of trading in 3 pillars: traders' psychology, technical analysis, and money management. This book is especially interesting for his psychological analysis of traders that will help prevent shortsighted behavior.

Leones contra gacelas (José Luis Cárpatos)

Purely speculative, albeit with a few lessons from fundamental analysis, in this book José Luis Carpathian shows his own tricks to win in the market and not to fall into the claws of the "lions." His description of what lurks behind every technical analysis signal and the market behaviors that generate them is especially interesting. Unfortunately, it is only available in Spanish at this time.

Stock Market Dictionary

Asset: good or right from which a company is to obtain a future benefit.

Balance Sheet: accounting statement that listed companies publish on a yearly basis to show their financial situation at year end.

Bearish trend: pattern in which prices are steadily dropping.

Blue-Chip: big and well-established company with important market share, steady incomes, and low volatility (for instance McDonald's, Coca-Cola...).

Broker: agent (individual or company) that acts as intermediary between a buyer and a seller, in this case between the investor/trader and the stock market.

Bullish trend: pattern in which prices are steadily increasing.

Capital: resources, assets or goods used to carry out a profitable activity, in this case the money we invest in stocks, bonds or other financial assets.

Capital gain: gain obtained from the sale of an asset at a higher price than it was purchased.

Chart: representation of the price of an asset over time.

Currency: local money that is exchanged in the market

Diversification: action of distributing investment in unrelated assets to reduce risk.

Dividend: amount of benefit that companies return to their shareholders.

Exchange rate: ratio between the values of different currencies. For example, the exchange rate between the euro and U.S. dollar (EUR/USD) is currently 1.28.

Financial products: assets whose price quotes in a regulated market such as the stock market.

Fundamental analysis: type of analysis that seeks to know the real value of a listed company by means of its statements.

Inflation: increase in the price of goods and services within a period of time.

Interest rate: cost of credit, i.e. percentage one has to pay to receive borrowed capital.

Liquidity: ease of conversion into money (by selling) an asset without losing value.

Long position: purchase of assets with the intention of ensuring profitability in the future by selling them at a higher price.

Portfolio: set of financial assets in which your capital has been invested (e.g., set of stocks in our holding).

Profitability: ability of an investment to generate profits.

Pull-back: eventual return of the price of an asset to its initial level after a strong turnaround.

P&L statement: document outlining the income and expenses of a company in a given period of time and revealing the origin of the losses or gains of a company.

Quote: Price that an asset (e.g., a stock) acquires in the market and that changes according to supply and demand.

Shares/Stocks: pieces of a listed company whose price quotes in the stock market.

Short position: sale of borrowed assets with the intention of buying them in the future at a lower price and returning them afterwards, thus obtaining a gain. It is possible to sell financial assets without having previously purchased them.

Sideways trend: pattern in which prices slightly vary, usually ranging between a minimum and a maximum value.

Technical analysis: type of analysis that utilizes price charts and trading volume data to foresee future price trends.

Technical indicator: statistical parameter calculated from past price and volume data which is intended to identify purchase and sale opportunities for an asset and to predict future price trends.

Trader: person that buys and sells assets for short-term profit.

Volatility: measure of the ability of an asset to abruptly change its market value (synonymous with risk).

Volume: amount of purchase-sale transactions on an asset that takes place over a period of time.

DISCLAIMER

All information contained in this book is original by the author. Charts were generated using graphical applications of the following websites: http://finance.yahoo.com and http://infobolsa.es/.

The reproduction, transmission or other use of the information contained in this book without explicit permission of the author is prohibited.

The author makes every effort to ensure the accuracy and timeliness of the information contained in this book. However, the author assumes no warranty or liability for the accuracy, completeness or suitability of the information contained or referenced in this book. Both access and use of the information contained or referenced in this book is under the sole responsibility and sole risk of the reader.

Neither the author nor any person or company involved in the creation, introduction of information or transmission of the information in this book assume liability for any damages arising from unauthorized access, use or any failure during use or any errors or omissions related with the content of the book.

Moreover, the author does not assume any responsibility for investments or unsuccessful transaction or losses arising from unauthorized access or any failure to use the content of this book.

The author does not encourage readers to make any particular financial investment/transaction but only provides them with means to perform their own analysis and make their own decisions based on consistent principles.